Date Due

MAR 28 1983			
JAN 28 1986			
JUL 0 2 1987			
MAR 13 1988			
DEC 28 89			
SEP 19 90			
OCT 3 91			
OCT 1 7 91			
DEC 02 91			

Contemporary Canadian Architecture

For our parents

EDWIN BERNSTEIN
PHYLLIS BERNSTEIN

EDGAR CAWKER
MARJORIE CAWKER

with love and gratitude

Contemporary
Canadian
Architecture
The Mainstream and Beyond

William Bernstein & Ruth Cawker

Fitzhenry & Whiteside
Toronto Montreal Winnipeg Vancouver

Cover design: Tiit Telmet of
            Gottshalk + Ash,
            International Design Consultants
Composition & Layout: Jay Tee Graphics Ltd.
Offset Lithography: Imprimerie Gagné

Fitzhenry & Whiteside Limited
150 Lesmill Road,
Don Mills, Ontario, Canada M3B 2T5

Published simultaneously in the United States of
America by Hastings House Inc.
ISBN 803-1281-7
and in the United Kingdom by Academy Editions.

Canadian Cataloguing in Publication Data
Bernstein, William, 1954-
    Contemporary Canadian architecture
Includes index.
Bibliography: p.
ISBN 0-88902-588-6

1. Architecture, Modern – 20th century – Canada.
I. Cawker, Ruth, 1953-   II. Title.
NA745.B47   724.9'1'0971   C81-094786-2

Library of Congress   82-83479

We would like to thank the Ontario Arts Council and
the Canada Council for their kind assistance in the
production of this book.

Printed in Canada

Contents

Preface

Recent years have seen an upsurge of interest in architecture across Canada. Naturally touched by events and publications in other English-speaking countries, Canadian architects, along with American, European, and Japanese architects, are re-evaluating the direction in which they have been moving and toward which they are heading in the future. Several developments — the foundation of the Canadian Architectural Archives in Calgary and of the Canadian Centre for Architecture in Montreal, the viability of new art/architecture bookstores, and Alcan's sponsorship of architectural lecture series in Montreal and Vancouver — attest to the willingness of Canadian architects to have an important presence in an increasingly vocal period of architecture.

What will hopefully emerge from this increase in theoretical activity surrounding architecture in Canada is a sense of the tradition of building and urban design at national and regional scales. Research into pre-war writings by architects like Percy Nobbs and John Lyle has already begun to unearth the roots of a distinctly Canadian architecture, one that is attuned to local characteristics of climate and culture. At the same time, studies in specific fields of Canadian art and culture provide a necessary counterpart to this growing historical awareness.

This book is an attempt to initiate a serious, informed, and prolonged discussion of modern architecture in Canada. Concentrating on major public commissions, we have selected projects built for and accessible to the general public. A thorough discussion of other areas, particularly housing, would have required another volume. Taking cognizance of the broadening interest in Canadian architecture, we have viewed the most significant directions of the years following the Expo '67 World Exposition in light of the historical and cultural contexts in which architecture has evolved. The book is organized into five interrelated sections to deal with these trends.

In the first chapter, Expo '67 is discussed as a manifestation of the heights to which liberalism ascended in the late 1960's in Canada. The architectural implications of individualism, egalitarianism, and internationalism are reviewed within the context of the fair and Canada's centennial year.

The focus of the second chapter is the 1976/77 competition for a new National Gallery in Ottawa. The mainstream of Canadian architecture is identified as a means of defining the norm in modern architectural practice. Entries to the competition are analyzed according to what their designs reveal of the aesthetic attitudes of the country's most established architects.

In contrast to Expo '67, and to architecture as an embodiment of liberalism, the third chapter examines the new conservatism and conservative attitudes towards culture and the environment. Major urban conservation projects in Halifax, Montreal, Ottawa, Toronto and Vancouver are discussed at length.

The fourth chapter looks at the impact of conservationist tendencies on large, *new* construction in Canada in recent years. Government-initiated guidelines, together with the popular appeal of rehabilitation and infill, have effected significant changes in the urban environment. Public space is the focus for examining the nature of these changes, which, in most cases, portend greater architectural awareness of social and cultural traditions.

The fifth and final section discusses the possibility of a reconciliation between the freedom of forms, materials and spaces inherent in the idea of a modern architecture, and the constructive attitudes towards the environment suggested by the new conservatism. Some of the strongest and most thoughtful recent buildings are discussed in this context.

Photography Credits

Arnott Rogers Batten Ltd., 83

Courtesy Archives Nationales, 70, 71, 72, 73, 74, 75

Bernstein, Cawker*, 40, 41, 43, 44, 45, 56, 58, 65, 67, 68, 69, 82, 84, 85, 86, 87, 92, 98, 102, 113, 127, 130, 131, 136, 140, 141, 142, 143, 156, 157, 158, 159, 160, 161, 168, 169, 170, 171, 172, 173, 176, 178, 184, 185, 186, 187, 188, 189, 190, 193, 198

Norman Cadorette, 119, 120

Foto Blohm & Assoc. Ltd., 8, 9, 10, 11, 12, 13, 14, 15, 16, 17, 18, 20, 21, 22, 23, 24, 25, 26, 27, 28, 29, 30, 31, 32, 33, 34, 35, 36, 37, 38, 39

© Melvin Charney, 76, 79, 80, 81

Graham French, 164

John Fulker, 132, 133, 134, 135, 137, 138, 194

Elizabeth Guilford, 46, 47, 48

Norman Hotson, 66

Jan Hughes, 95, 96, 97

Balthazar Korab, courtesy of I. M. Pei & Partners, 125

Marc Lullier, 118

Miller Services/H. Armstrong Roberts, 1

Miller Services/National Film Board, 2

Courtesy National Capital Commission, 51, 52, 53, 54

Courtesy North Shore Archives, 129

NFB Photothèque ONF/Ted Grant, 3

Panda Associates, 60, 114

Courtesy, I. M. Pei & Partners, 123, 124

© Retoria: Y. Futagawa & Assoc. Photographers; Photo by Y. Takasu, 192, 195, 196

Ian Samson, 111, 112, 115, 116, 179, 180, 197

Simon Scott, 63, 64

© Ezra Stoller ESTO, 105, 106, 107, 108, 109, 122

Ezra Stoller, courtesy of I. M. Pei & Partners, 126, 128

Gabor Szilasi, 77, 78

Peter Tittenberger, 144, 146, 150, 151, 152, 154, 183

Courtesy Toronto Transit Commission, 93, 94, 101, 103

University of Winnipeg Graphics Department, 181, 182

Ron Vickers Ltd., 6

The publisher would like to thank the following for granting permission to reprint previously published images:

Institute for Architecture and Urban Studies, Figure 7, reprinted from *Philip Johnson: Processes*. Craig Owens and Giorgio Ciucci, Catalogue No. 9, 1978.

Architecture + Urbanism (Japan) and H. Hertberger, Figure 19, reprinted from March 1977, Volume No. 75.

Figure 90, reprinted from *Delirious New York*, Rem Koolhaas, Oxford University Press, 1978.

Joyce E. Morrow, Figure 91, reprinted from *Calgary, Many Years Hence*, Joyce Morrow, University of Calgary, 1979.

*Printed by Panda Associates

Acknowledgments

First and foremost, we are indebted to William Dendy and Penina Coopersmith for their continued and vital support. By providing historical background, and by making available his own research into preservation, banks and museum architecture, Bill Dendy played a key role in the development of the book. Penina Coopersmith, with her involvement in planning and architectural journalism, helped to pinpoint and clarify the issues we felt were central to the text.

We would also like to acknowledge the assistance of the Canada Council and the Ontario Arts Council; grants from both agencies made possible the travel, research, and much of the photography for the preparation of this book.

In the course of our travels we were directed, advised, and encouraged by many people.

In Victoria, we would like to thank Dan Savard.

In Vancouver, we were assisted by Michael Ames, Gerry Brewer, Robert Collier, Arthur Davies, Barry Downs, Arthur Erickson, Rainer Fassler, Richard Henriquez and Bill McLennan.

In Edmonton, Douglas Cardinal; Doug, Glen and Monty Cawker; Richard Schick and Joseph Shoctor were of great assistance.

In Ponoka, thanks to Ed Clarke.

In Calgary, we express much gratitude to Michael McMordie, Harold Hanen and Jack Long.

In Saskatoon, but now in Victoria, greetings and thanks to Margery Fee.

In Winnipeg, we would like to thank J. M. Badertscher, Lionel Ditz, Etienne Gaboury, J. G. Pincock, Gustavo da Roza, Michael Rattray and Peter Tittenberger.

In Toronto, we express our gratitude to George Baird, Hans Blumenfeld, Charles Cansfield, Donald Clinton, Howard Cohen, Paul Cravit, A. J. Diamond, Ronald Dick, Dan Dunlop, Oscar Duskes, Robert Fitzhenry, Susan Ford, Robert Hill, Robert Hopewell, Jan Hughes, Helen Katz, Michael Kirkland, Eileen Mak, Pamela Manson-Smith, Joe Medjuk, the Department of Fine Arts at the Metropolitan Library, C. Blake Millar, Raymond Moriyama, Barton Myers, John C. Parkin, Hugh Robertson, Frederick Rounthwaite, Helen Sinclair, Lorne Tepperman, Don Schmidt, Tim Shortreed, Peter Silcox, Heather Strongitharm, G. S. Vickers, Ted Wickson, Caroline Walker, Arthur Wood, and Boris Zerafa.

In Ottawa, gratitude is due: Arthur Capling, Guy Desbarats, Mirjana Lakich, Claude Lavoie, Gyde Sheperd and Dr. H'sio Yen-shih.

In Montreal, we were assisted by Ray Affleck, André Blouin, Melvin Charney, Céline Larivière, Peter Rose, Victor Prus and Jacques Reeves.

In Halifax, thanks to Allen Duffus, Elizabeth Guilford and Tony Jackson.

In New York, our thanks go out to Edwin and James Bernstein, Robbie Jamieson, Nancy Hahn, Jean Roberge, Erica Stoller and Nigel Thompson.

I   *Terre des Hommes*

To the more than fifty million people who came to visit it, Expo '67 presented an unforgettable picture of Canada at a particular stage in its growth as a nation. In keeping with the country's internationalist, peace keeping self-image in the 1960's, Canada's unique history and culture were downplayed. Instead, the emphasis was on a kind of perfect, state-less individual and a world wherein such individuals were equal. There was little room for the equally important collective and hierarchical values of Canadian society. All this was made abundantly clear through the environmental medium of the fair, the temporary city that was Expo '67.

One of the earliest decisions made in planning the fair was the choice of "Terre des Hommes" as its theme. The title of one of Antoine de Saint Exupéry's books, *Terre des Hommes*, told the story of France's first generation of commercial aviators, and the dangers and risks associated with their trade. Roughly translated into English as "Man and His World," it was up to a meeting of intellectuals to make of the book a theme for a world's fair.

A "theme-meeting" was held in Montebello, Quebec in 1963, attended by architects, lawyers, artists, authors and, strangely enough, a neurosurgeon. Responding to the theme of heroic individualism underlying Saint-Exupéry's depiction of the first generation of commercial aviators, the conference proposed that the fair celebrate the place and potential of the individual in a world of progress and change. In this regard, Saint-Exupéry was quoted: "To be a man is to feel that one's own stone contributes to building the edifice of the world."

To this emphasis on the individual was added its corollary in liberal thought: equality among individuals. Author Gabrielle Roy, one of the participants at the conference, summed up the group's "one firm basis of accord" as "faith in progress," but further explained the concept of progress in egalitarian terms, as opposed to the more usual scientific ones. "Progress," explained Roy, "should signify an increasingly equitable human distribution of misfortune and advantage. To progress then would mean to work towards a gradual '*rapprochement*' of all men of every condition and origin."

Saint-Exupéry, however, did not depict *all* men as heroic individuals; in *Terre des Hommes* aviators are, but bureaucrats are not. In choosing to quote Saint-Exupéry, the conferees had to do so quite carefully and selectively. For example, Saint-Exupéry had written of freedom that it "leads to equality, and equality leads to equilibrium, which is death." "If there is no hierarchy," he wrote elsewhere, "there is no brotherhood."

Most significant in the theme for the fair which emerged from the conference was its purposeful omission of nationalistic sentiment. Despite the fact that it was Canada's hundredth birthday, Expo '67 was not to explicitly promote or celebrate *Canada* (or any other nation for that matter); the theme of the fair was to be, at once, the individual and the world at large, with very little in-between. "The entire development," concluded the conference, "shall reflect the primacy given to human values and apirations in the theme '*Terre des Hommes.*' It must not be presented as a '*terre des nations*' or a '*terre des machines.*' "

Physical planning for Expo '67 began in the same year as the Montebello Conference, 1963. Initially, the team of planners hired by the exhibition corporation proposed that the fair be located within the city of Montreal. As part of this proposal, experimental housing projects were to be built in various derelict areas of the city, hopefully to act as catalysts for future revitalization.

But poor and run-down urban areas were not part of the successful and exciting image of Montreal that Mayor Jean Drapeau wanted to project to the rest of the world. Instead, Drapeau proposed that the fair be located on an island in Montreal's harbour, Ile Sainte-Hélène. When it became apparent that this island alone was not large enough to accommodate the fair, a new island was created alongside, and named Ile Nôtre-Dame. Thus, the site for Expo '67 was established: isolated by water from Montreal, but with it in view, the city was to serve as a backdrop against which the fair could unfold.

Thus, planning took a very different course than it would have, had the fair been integrated into the existing city fabric. The planners severed ties with traditional urban planning and struck out on their own to create a three-dimensional organization appropriate to "an age of sophisticated technological advances." The search began, not for a "town plan," as had been the case with previous world fairs, but rather for what was termed a "framework of orientation."

As opposed to a traditional town plan, which relies on a hierarchy of *spaces*, in terms of squares and streets, to organize the environment, the planners of Expo '67 envisioned a hierarchy of *transportation systems* to organize the fair. The primary means of transportation was to be a silver express train called the "Expo Express" which would bring visitors into, through and out of the two islands in twenty minutes if they did not get off. The Expo Express stopped at only four points within the fair, points which the planners termed "nodes." The secondary system of transportation was

to be a monorail which travelled in loops, originating and terminating at the "nodes." Significantly, the overall organization of Expo was not to be understood as the visitor walked in and through it but, rather, from above, and at a speed of forty kilometres an hour (twenty-five miles an hour) whilst seated comfortably on the mostly-elevated Expo Express.

Four theme pavilions, representing Man the Explorer, Man the Producer, Man the Provider and Man in the Community, were to be built in conjunction with the nodes, in order to further develop these points as centres of the fair. The smaller pavilions were supposed to plug-into the theme pavilions, in the best tradition of the English architecture group Archigram's "plug-in city." Participation was not obligatory but those that opted to plug-in were permitted a "choice of

Figure 1. Aerial view of Expo '67, Montreal, with Ile Sainte-Hélène in the foreground and Ile Notre-Dame in the background.

Figure 2. Expo '67, Montreal, part of the transportation system with Montreal in the background.

location and environment and allowed . . . free expression." The aim was to devise a framework which would "free the individual to contribute to the pattern rather than be imprisoned by it."

As actually built, the smaller industrial and national pavilions bore only a tangential relationship to the larger theme pavilions in their general area. Sites were limited by coverage restrictions to a minimum of 40% and a maximum of 60%. There were also height limitations on some of the pavilions, according to location. In terms of architectural style or expression, there were no real limits or restrictions; architects were "asked" to "explore the possibilities of web or film-like materials stretched over bold frames or the frank assembly of mass-produced components fastened together in patternful ways . . . " (*Figures 1,2*)

Figure 3. Expo '67, Man the Producer Pavilion, Ile Notre-Dame. Affleck Desbarats Dimakopoulos Lebensold and Sise, Architects.

Like the planners of the fair, the architects of the individual pavilions seemed intent on searching out new and experimental architectural solutions wherever possible. Man the Producer and Man the Explorer (both by Affleck, Desbarats, Dimakopoulos, Lebensold and Sise), the theme pavilions on Ile Nôtre-Dame and Ile St. Hélène respectively, were both constructed out of identically-sized tetrahedra (three-dimensional structural forms). *(Figure 3)*

The U.S. pavilion, a geodesic dome by Buckminster Fuller, was also built out of metal piping but the structure as a whole was much more complicated. In fact, the sizes and connections of metal piping required to make this "simple" geometric form were so complex that the design could be carried out only with the aid of a computer. *(Figure 4)*

The use of a computer seemed to confer a certain distinction on the designer; one architect boasted that

Figure 4. Expo '67, The United States Pavilion. Buckminster Fuller, Architect.

the structure of his pavilion was so complex that it required two hours of computer analysis, as opposed to 30,000 man-lifetimes of manual arithmetic. Apparently, pavilion design, in itself, was simply not challenging enough. The German Pavilion, in which a large, curling, steel mesh roof was hung from eight supports, could have been fifty times larger than it was without changing its design, according to Frei Otto, the architect.

Blurring the distinctions between traditional parts of buildings — between door and window, front and back, and from one room to the next — was another Expo '67 hallmark. In the German Pavilion, even the distinction between inside and outside was subtle.

To architects and non-architects alike, the fair represented a welcome departure from the boring and monotonous box-like character of modern architecture. Journalist Robert Fulford commented:

At Expo the walls slanted. Doors and windows were, quite often, not rectangular. The right angle and the straight line no longer ruled the world — there were hexagons, pentagons and truncated tetrahedrons. Not everything was made of steel and glass: there were plastics, too, and plywoods . . . . There was so much that was fresh and different and even daring that it seemed a new world of architectural design was opening up; and some of us imagined that we might even be in at the beginning of a revolution.

Architects, and especially architectural critics, were not always as willing to whole-heartedly endorse the "anything-goes" approach to the environment represented by Expo. The editor of *Progressive Architecture*, Jan Rowan, coined the phrase "no-space spaces" to describe the oft-repeated sensation, once inside many of the pavilions, of total darkness relieved only by the light of a spotlight or film projector.

"Besides no-space spaces," commented Rowan in an editorial on Expo, "what an architect will notice at Expo . . . is the discontinuity of experience." To many visitors, this very feeling was part of the overall excitement which was to be expected at a world's fair. But to many architects and planners, anxious about the increasing discontinuity between one modern building and the next (something which was especially noticeable in an urban context), the fair represented a dangerous tendency of modern architecture.

Previewing the Expo construction site in 1966, architectural critic Peter Collins wrote:

> If Canada had really wanted to give a lead in planning its celebration of Canadian unity, it might profitably have empowered the Chief Architect of Expo '67 to impose complete co-ordination in the design of each pavilion and, consequently, in the detailed design of the spaces and relationships between them. . . . I would have infinitely preferred a totally integrated environment to the disparate miscellany which the partly-finished carcases portend.

A year before the fair had opened, Professor Collins had noted not only the eventual unrelatedness of the Expo environment but also the unusual way that Canada had chosen to celebrate its hundredth birthday. Not that having the exposition to mark the event was unusual; the United States had done the same thing in Philadelphia on its centennial in 1876 and many of the world's fairs have marked one type of anniversary or another. What was unusual was that, unlike previous fairs, and Expo '70 in Osaka, Canada played down Expo as a specifically Canadian event in favour of stressing that which all men (as opposed to nations) shared in common: Man the Producer; Man the Explorer etc. The Canadian Pavilion, which might in other circumstances have been the centrepiece of the fair, was placed off at one end of Ile Nôtre-Dame, overshadowed by the "universal" theme pavilions and other national pavilions with more presence. Rather than distinguishing Canada as a nation, from other nations, the fair proved that Canadians were just like everyone else. Put another way, Canada was just as *modern* as anyplace else. On opening day, journalist Peter Newman wrote:

> The cannonade of fireworks which marked the opening of Expo may in retrospect turn out to have been one of those rare moments that change the direction of a nation's history . . . surely the modernization of Canada — of its skylines, of its styles, its institutions — will be dated from this occasion and from this fair . . . .

Eager to shed its isolated and provincial image, Canada utilized its centennial to thrust itself into the realm of international achievement, culture and architecture. The mood was one of optimism, expansiveness and the then-pleasant sensation of flux and change.

II The Classic Solution: Mainstream Architecture in Canada

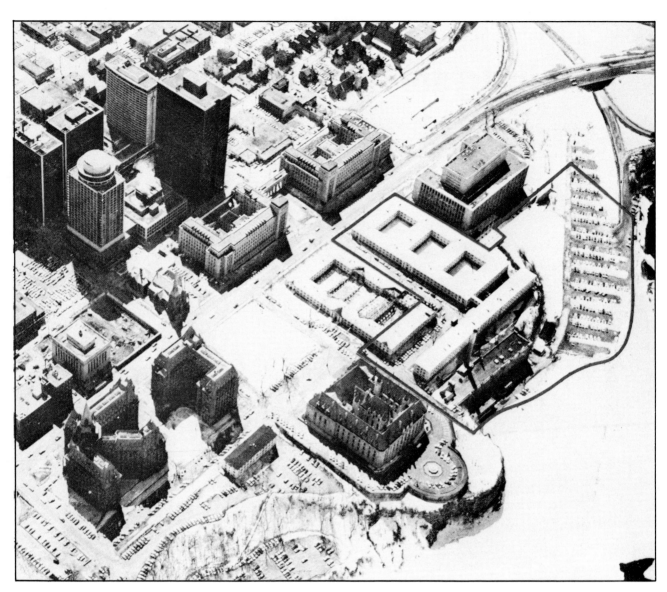

Figure 5. The National Gallery Competition, 1976, Ottawa, Wellington Street site. The site is outlined by a black border. All structures on the site, with the exception of the Cliff Street powerplant (with smokestack), have been demolished.

Almost a decade following Expo, the opportunity to monumentalize another important centennial gave rise to a design competition for a new National Gallery of Canada. Sponsored by the Department of Public Works on the basis of a programme prepared by the National Gallery and endorsed by the National Capital Commission, the competition showed what had become of the modernization of styles and institutions in Canada.

As in other architectural competitions, the 1976/77 National Gallery competition was intended to elicit a variety of proposals for a specific building, and to choose the best among them. Not unlike the planning and design process for Expo '67, the competition was viewed as a means of involving both the architectural profession and the public in a cultural event of national importance. And as competitions typically inspire architects, the National Gallery competition was expected to result in a building of exceptional merit. For a large public agency like the Department of Public Works, the anonymity of the competition process guaranteed impartiality. A competition promised to be the one means of selecting an architect that would be as attractive to the public as it was to the architectural profession. *(Figure 5)*

The failure of the 1976/77 National Gallery competition to bestow the intended benefits on its sponsor, its participants, or even its winner, demonstrates poignantly the hazards of the competition process. Even more importantly, however, the competition demonstrated the interrelationship between architecture, art and prevailing cultural attitudes. By attracting many of the country's most successful firms the competition provided a unique opportunity to evaluate mainstream architectural practice and aesthetic principles.

The first stage of the competition was an elaborate screening process, intended to ensure that the winning competitor would be able to carry out the work required for the $80 million building without going bankrupt. Architects found that they had to team up with other firms of architects or consultants to produce the required assurances and a guarantee of sufficient experience. A few statements about the firm's approach to designing the nation's new art gallery were also requested, but the stringent and point-rated financial requirements, coupled with the necessary proof of analogous design experience, effectively screened out young, inexperienced firms. Design ability, in the competition's first stage, was merely a matter of track record.

Despite vigorous protest over the bias toward large and very experienced firms, the first stage proceeded as

the Department of Public Works (DPW) intended. Of the 456 architects and architectural firms who indicated interest when the competition was announced, only 56 replied to the brochure outlining the selection process. These submissions represented 89 architectural firms and over 300 engineering and consulting groups from seven provinces. Of the 56 first-stage competitors, ten firms, the vast majority of them based in Toronto and Montréal, survived the qualification standards to procede to stage two. Stage two was the real competition, for which competitors were sent a programme listing all the requirements for the preparation of designs for the National Gallery's building.

Significantly, eight of the second-stage competitors had appeared on a short-list of twelve firms drawn up by DPW before the decision to hold a competition had been made. Compared to the practice of Europe, Scandinavia, and Japan, where competitions provide even the most inexperienced or radical architects with fairly unrestricted opportunities to express their design ideas, the National Gallery competition seemed instead to be calculated to involve only the most established architectural firms. The ten names at the starting line for the second stage design competition were:

> ARCOP Associates, Montreal, with Jodoin Lamarre Pratte, Montreal;
> Bregman & Hamann, Don Mills, with C. Blake Millar, Toronto;
> Gustavo da Roza, Architect, Winnipeg, with Number Ten Architectural Group, Architects & Planners, Winnipeg;
> Arthur Erickson, Toronto and Vancouver, with David Boulva Cleve, Montreal;
> Raymond Moriyama, Architects & Planners, Toronto;
> Parkin Architects & Planners, Toronto;
> Victor Prus, Architect & Urbanist, Montreal, with Bland Lemoyne Shine Lacroix, Architectes et Urbanistes, Montreal, with Longpré Marchand Goudreau Dobush Stewart Hein, Architects, Montreal, with Hébert Lalonde, Architectes, Montréal;
> Webb Zerafa Menkès Housden Partnership, Architects & Engineers, Toronto;
> Wiens and Associates Ltd., Regina, with Marani Rounthwaite & Dick, Architects & Engineers, Toronto;
> Zeidler Partnership, Architects, Toronto.

These long-established and financially successful firms, DPW decided, were the ones most capable of designing and producing the National Gallery's building without creating the kind of cost overruns that had made the Sydney Opera House a national political fiasco.

Figure 6. The Toronto-Dominion Centre, Toronto. John B. Parkin Associates/Bregmam & Hamann Architects; Engineers, Planners; Mies van der Rohe, Consultant.

Figure 7. The A. T. & T. Corporate Headquarters, New York. Johnson/Burgee Architects, Simmons Architects.

Guy Desbarats, Assistant Deputy Minister of DPW, was the first to promote the idea of holding this particular competition. The national prominence achieved by the Montreal-based firm of Affleck, Desbarats, Dimakopoulos, Lebensold, Michaud, and Sise (ARCOP now), in which he had been a partner, derived in large measure from its competition victories for the National Arts Centre in Ottawa and Place des Arts in Montreal. In his own words, "The whole point of the competition was fairness — to remove the burden of decision-making from the public servant and put it in the hands of an impartial jury."

Gyde Shepherd, Assistant Director of the National Gallery and project leader for the new building, suggested that the competition represented a compromise between Mr. Desbarats' department and the Museums Corporation. His view was that, "There wouldn't have been agreement between DPW and Museums over a choice of architect. The choice was made for them by the competition."

One purpose of staging the competition in two steps was to obtain a short list of competitors which would include architects favoured by both agencies. John C. Parkin, whose firm won the competition's second stage, explained what the stage two competitors had in common, describing them as "a group of highly competitive people, all of whom are very close friends . . . . Most of us started off in the immediate post-War period and were among the pioneers of the post-War period of building in Canada . . . . Chronologically we are not young men, but I think we still are very much in a position of creating what is acceptable in Canada today."

Parkin, who prefers to identify his own firm's work as "mainstream twentieth-century architecture," rather than as the currently pejorative "International Style," has given a number of speeches in which the goals of "the mainstream" are spelled out. An honours graduate from Harvard's Masters programme in architecture in 1947, John Parkin came into contact with such well-known Modernists as Walter Gropius, Marcel Breuer, and Le Corbusier. His earlier partnership with John B. Parkin (no family relation) was one of the first Canadian firms to carry out the reductive, abstracted principles made popular a generation earlier in Europe. Two of the best-known buildings executed by his firm were in fact done in association with architects of the Modern Movement: Toronto City Hall was built with the late Finnish architect, Viljo Rewell; and the Toronto Dominion Centre was designed by Mies van der Rohe. Many of his firm's early buildings, not least his own house, were patterned on Miesian models. *(Figure 6)*

In the many texts and articles about the Modern Movement, however, John Parkin's name is never mentioned. And his co-competitors in the National Gallery competition, with few exceptions, remain largely unheard-of, even in Canada. A possible explanation for their anonymity is that the Canadian mainstream architects were not (like Walter Gropius or Mies van der Rohe, the original "Pioneers of the Modern Movement" discussed in Nicholas Pevsner's book of the same title) at the vanguard of a revolution in architectural style.

Rather, they were pioneers of a revolution in architectural practice that accompanied the post-War building boom in North America. The Canadian mainstream is more truly contemporary with, and sympathetic to, the generation of American Modernists who studied architecture under the original "Pioneers": Kevin Roche, I. M. Pei, Paul Rudolph, and Cesar Pelli. Like this "second generation" of American Modern architects, the more senior competitors of the National Gallery competition's second stage — Ray Affleck, Sidney Bregman, John Parkin, and Boris Zerafa — have seen their own practices grow, and sometimes retract, in tandem with the patronage of large development companies and corporations.

The most noticeable quality of mainstream architecture, reflecting the fundamental objectives of its patrons, is an unadorned structural efficiency. In this, many Canadian architects differ from their American counterparts whose attempts to evoke styles of the past have been widely publicized. John Parkin, not alone amongst his co-competitors in criticizing Philip Johnson's A.T. & T. building in New York, summarized their objections:

> Philip said in 1960, "Let's enjoy the foggy chaos of it all." The public is not interested in "the foggy chaos." They want amenable buildings, they want practical buildings that work, buildings that are comfortable and pleasurable. They're not interested in the Chippendale armoire style. *(Figure 7)*

A second quality of mainstream architecture, one which is really an extension of the first, is the emphasis of basic building units for rhetorical effect. Again, this quality helps to distinguish the Canadian mainstream from its American counterpart. For while American clients, being most frequently private and highly competitive corporations, favour the imagability provided by super-star architectural firms, the clientele for Canadian architecture is largely comprised of near-monopolies: Canadian banks, developers, telephone and utility companies, and the Federal Government, to name a few.

A typical Canadian client of mainstream architecture like DPW, in contrast to an American one, prefers to work with balanced, interdisciplinary teams of architects, engineers, and cost consultants, which are headed by skillful administrators of moderate ambition. "This century," Guy Desbarats feels, "has overrated the nineteenth-century ideal of the individual."

Reluctant to cultivate an architecture of personality, the Canadian mainstream has tended to avoid making explicit symbols in buildings, opting instead for the formally neutral devices of proportion and scale. A good example of the type of project the Canadian mainstream cut its teeth on is the Toronto-Dominion Centre shown earlier. Far from advertising its presence, the complex's main banking hall is housed in a pavilion which is identical in colour, material, and detail to the nearby office towers. Only its privileged corner location on the vast site suggests that it is the T-D Bank's head branch.

John Parkin, whose firm executed Mies van der Rohe's design for the Centre, feels that, "Architects should be relatively anonymous people, working and doing a good job for people. We have to refine, and avoid digressions that are just fashions created by editors' need for cult figures. Canadians don't need a Man of the Year." In the tradition of Expo '67, mainstream architecture made tangible the ascending liberal post-War society with its collective social order. Erickson/Massey's Simon Fraser campus, Affleck et. al.'s Place Bonaventure, Webb Zerafa Menkès Housden's original design for Lothian Mews, and Zeidler's Ontario Place are all works that prefigured the advance of an increasingly prosperous and egalitarian society.

However, by the time DPW announced its intention to hold a competition for the National Gallery, economic conditions had changed and, with them, the standards for what could be feasibly constructed. The wage and price controls imposed during the Federal Government's 1975 economic austerity programme signalled the end of unbridled expansion. Coming shortly after cutbacks in museum funding, the National Gallery competition's terms of reference underscored the importance of staying on target with cost and scheduling.

The eight hundred-page programme distributed to the stage two competitors spelt out in very specific terms what was required: the functions, dimensions, and interrelationships of each room of the National Gallery were presented as inflexible guidelines. Urban design requirements were predicated on an "urban space system" of new pedestrian paths linking the gallery site to adjacent buildings. Format requirements indicated exactly the scales, types, and numbers of drawings and models required to judge the submissions. No colour, in fact no shading, was allowed on the presentation panels.

By suppressing many possible means of individual expression, the competition rules contributed greatly to the similarity of the ultimate submissions. Guy Desbarats, despite his avowed enthusiasm for competitions, felt apprehensive about the context of federal economic restraint.

> Competitions add cost to architecture, but they also add time, which is even more important. To get a project going within the life of one government is very dicey. If a competition adds a year to the process, it can make the difference between it taking off and it not taking off.

The process of site selection had already limited the Gallery's own expectations for its future. The site DPW chose was on the Ottawa River at the west end of Wellington Street between the Supreme Court and the National Library, hardly booming tourist attractions. Jean Sutherland Boggs, the Gallery's Director from 1966 to 1976, made her preference for locating the Gallery on Cartier Square abundantly clear. Cartier Square is close to the Lorne Building where the Gallery is currently housed. This site would have facilitated the move of the Gallery's collection and, more important, it is immediately adjacent to the National Arts Centre, at the busy hub of downtown Ottawa. The site would have ensured a high profile and, correspondingly, the popularity which has made recent American galleries, notably the National Gallery in Washington, D.C., into national attractions.

Jean Boggs campaigned vigorously against the choice of the Wellington Street site, arguing that it was too small, too out-of-the-way, and that it was needed for National Library expansion. To the Gallery's staff, the Wellington Street site, with its view across the river to new government office and apartment towers in downtown Hull and its proximity to the Portage Bridge, seemed to have the taint of a political gesture.

Due to the Gallery's absorption in 1968 into the Museums Corporation, an umbrella organization overseeing all the national museums, Jean Boggs was as powerless in reversing the decision to locate the building at the quiet end of Wellington Street as she had been in implementing a multitude of decisions affecting budgeting and the day-to-day affairs of the Gallery. Her subsequent acceptance of an academic post at Harvard seemed also a political gesture, directed angrily at the Museums Corporation. A scant five weeks before the

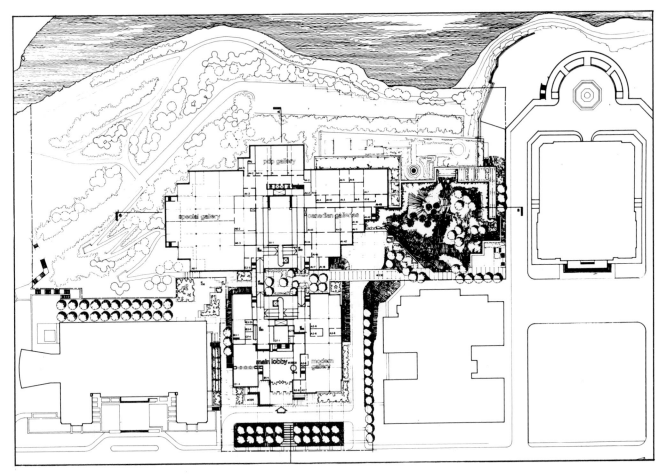

Figure 8. National Gallery, Ottawa, Site plan. ARCOP
Associates, Montreal, with Jodoin Lamarre Pratte.

jury was to choose one of the ten submissions Jean
Boggs left Ottawa.

The development of the programme with which
competitors would have to work became an even greater
exercise in constrait for both the Gallery and the
entrants. The programme Jean Boggs and her staff had
devised prior to her decision to resign would have made
the Gallery "an illustrated book of the history of art,"
according to G. S. Vickers, an art historian and friend
of Boggs, who was named to the competition jury. This
idealistic programme was subsequently edited by the
Museums Corporation, according to the directions of
the Treasury Board. Then professional programmers,
Philip Bobrow & Associates, reworked the inventory of
requirements into the final documents issued for the
second stage. Their extreme detail was intended to
emphasize the cost restrictions for the resulting
building.

The syllabus of spaces and facilities required for
the new Gallery was, for most second-stage competitors, the most contentious aspect of the competition.
The firm of Webb Zerafa Menkès Housden had a
special team that did nothing else but decipher the programme. Some firms hired outside consultants and
computer time. Those who opted to figure it out for
themselves generally agreed with Fred Rounthwaite's
assessment (Marani Rounthwaite & Dick) that "doing
the adjacencies (i.e., the relationship of required spaces
and facilities) was like doing a jigsaw with pieces that
didn't fit." The often picayune and sometimes conflicting requirements made the second stage into a very
expensive proposition. Blake Millar claimed that he per-
sonally logged over 1600 hours in the four-month time
period of the competition. (On a daily basis, Millar's
estimate works out to over 13 hours per working day,
not allowing for a single day off.) "I didn't even recog-

Figure 9. National Gallery, Model, River view. ARCOP team proposal.

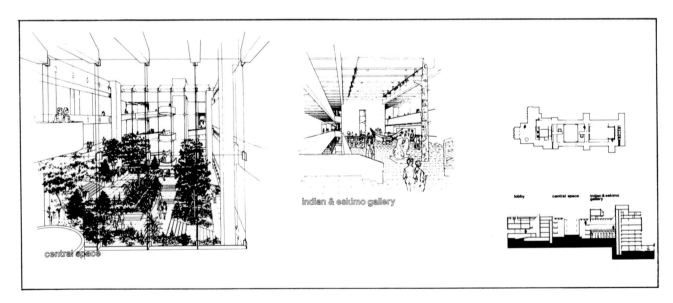

Figure 10. National Gallery, Ottawa, drawings showing location and character of the central atrium and a typical gallery space. ARCOP team proposal.

nize my family nor they me,'' he claimed. ''It was a matter of almost total isolation to organize all the facets of the work and to bring it all together . . . . At a normal hourly rate for salary, we certainly would have logged well over $200,000 worth of time and were paid $35,000 to include all expenses.''

The competing teams devoted much of their attention to solving the functional problems of arranging the Gallery's services, with the result that many of the designs can not be readily appreciated unless one understands the intricacies of the programme. Almost half of the competitors designed buildings that were intended to be no more than backgrounds for the nation's art collection. These four designs are studied here as a group, for their flexible, ''universal'' qualities reveal that most basic trait of mainstream architecture: the reduction of building to a rational system.

The entries submitted by Victor Prus, Raymond Moriyama, and Arthur Erickson point in a somewhat different direction. Appearing to mimic the surrounding landscape, these three entries represent the American mainstream trend of imposing incisive forms onto otherwise ''universal'' interior spaces.

A third group of entries seems to address the most ambitious, and also one of the most obscurely-stated objectives of the programme, namely to design a building ''which, while it responds to other necessary functions, is an architectural analogue to the art it contains.'' As a result, the Gallery designs submitted by Blake Millar, Gustavo da Rosa, and Eberhard Zeidler are provocative aesthetic statements in their own right, challenging the well-established limits of mainstream design.

Architects in the first group, which includes the Parkin Partnership's winning design, reacted to the stringency of the guidelines by taking an approach of extreme caution: what was wanted was a neutral background against which objects singled out as Art could be displayed. Boris Zerafa of the Webb Zerafa Menkès Housden Partnership (WZMH), himself an art collector, summarized the ''background'' attitude: ''The building had almost to be a non-building. The architect had to take a subdued second role . . . . It was a matter of creating a space or an enclosure that allowed one to relax and enjoy the piece of art in question.'' Of his firm's submissions, he explained, ''Taking cognizance of the siting and the importance of the building relative to the national capital, we came up with a very simpli-fied solution that was dignified but actually was a non-building from the street side. And internally it was to strictly focus on the art itself.''

The first group of competitors shared this view of the building as a neutral container for works of art, a view essentially derived from such museum designs as Mies van der Rohe's Museum for a Small City (1942) and his National Gallery in Berlin (1968). But while Mies van der Rohe's early museums and exhibition pavilions were bold demonstrations of a new minimalist architectural aesthetic, the ''background'' schemes had the effect of removing aesthetics from the architecture, for fear of its clashing with the art.

Unlike many of their American counterparts, most Canadian mainstream architects have avoided involvement in current controversies over style, maintaining a functionalism that is detached from aesthetics. A former teacher and frequent lecturer, John Parkin has come to feel that:

> Architecture is not an opening night issue. Architecture is something that has to be understood and recreated through the passage of time. I don't countenance or pay any attention to criticism of any building if the criticism is founded upon one's perception a month or so after opening . . . . I am very interested in the criticism that is now emerging of buildings built ten or fifteen years ago.

For both ARCOP Associates' and Clifford Wiens & Associates/Marani Rounthwaite Dick's schemes, the subordination of the environment to the experience of art meant that circulation through the interior spaces of the building was stressed. Particularly in the ARCOP scheme, the emphasis on a clear path of movement, from the major public facilities at the southern entrance to the galleries to the north, provided the plan with its rational order. Consequently, the main interior space was to be the intersection of this north-south path and a required pedestrian mall linking the Gallery to other institutions on Parliament Hill to the east. The prime purpose of this space, an outdoor court planted with native trees, was to orient the visitor by means of views of the various surrounding building parts, and beyond the building to the river and the Parliament Hill landmarks. As for the exterior facades of the building, a very restrained facade greeted Wellington Street, while hooded, jagged masses were grouped on the north side, overlooking the dramatic slope of the cliff. *(Figures 8, 9, 10)*

Figure 11. National Gallery, Model, River view. Wiens team proposal.

Figure 12. National Gallery, Model, Aerial view. Wiens team proposal.

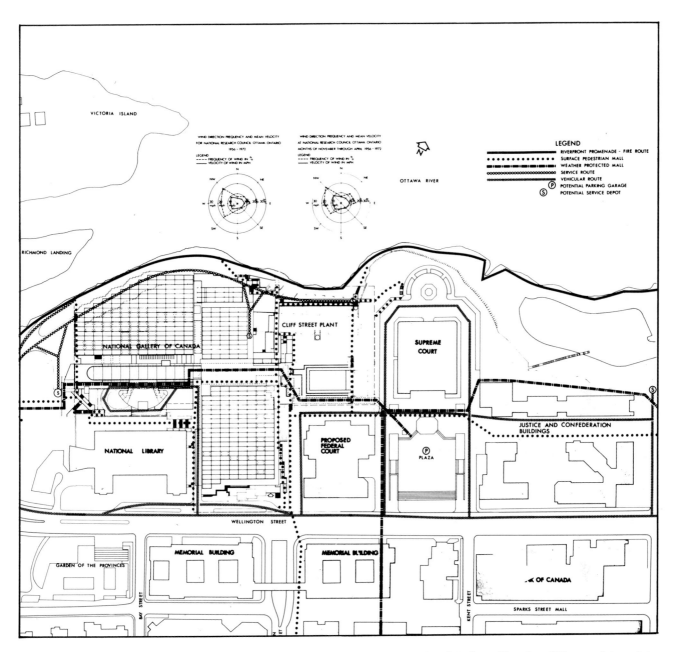

Figure 13. National Gallery, Site plan. Wiens and Associates Ltd., with Marani Rounthwaite & Dick.

Similarly, the Clifford Wiens & Associates/MRD team proposed a central focus at the junction of two main paths. The site was blanketed by a ground-hugging structure, with its river edge roughly serrated to approximate the cliff's contours. On the outside, the building appeared to conform to the landscape. Mirrored grey glass, granite, and concrete tinted to match the cliff further effaced the Gallery's low form. *(Figures 11,12,13)*

Figure 14. National Gallery, Model, Aerial view. The Webb
Zerafa Menkes Housden Partnership (WZMH).

At least two firms in this first group held in-house
competitions to choose a design. WZMH pitted three
younger members of the firm against Boris Zerafa. By
his own account, Zerafa designed a "sculptural"
building that did not conform strictly to the programme. However, afraid of being disqualified, his
partners favoured, and ultimately submitted one of the
younger architect's more neutral designs. The neutral
design had a somewhat ambiguous exterior image; a
"background" of whitish marble by day, the building at
night exhibited the brightly-painted ductwork inside its
perimeter, by means of floodlights shining out through
the transluscent stone cladding. Natural light was to
enter gallery spaces via motor-shuttered skylights. These
funnel-shaped skylights lent visual rhythm to the
building's whitish exterior. *(Figures 14, 15, 16)*

The WZMH design team had a score sheet with all
of the programme requirements assigned points. "We
certainly felt the more neutral scheme achieved 99.99%

of all the points," Boris Zerafa reflected. "The winning
design deviated from the programme. Parkin had the
guts to do this and that is why he deserved to win."

The Parkin Partnership's winning scheme was
chosen, not according to the extent to which it met the
mandatory requirements (the scheme violated certain
stipulations, including those for school bus access), but
because it provided an unmistakable order, a kind of
generalized system for displaying and viewing art. In the
words of the jury's final report, the Parkin scheme was
chosen for "its major virtue. [The scheme] distinguishes
itself from the other competitors' by its sense of order."
Several competitors complained after the competition
that adherence to the programme cost them time,
money, and most bitterly, a shot at first prize. One competitor went so far as to contact principals of several
teams with the idea of suing the government, an idea
which obviously never came to fruition.

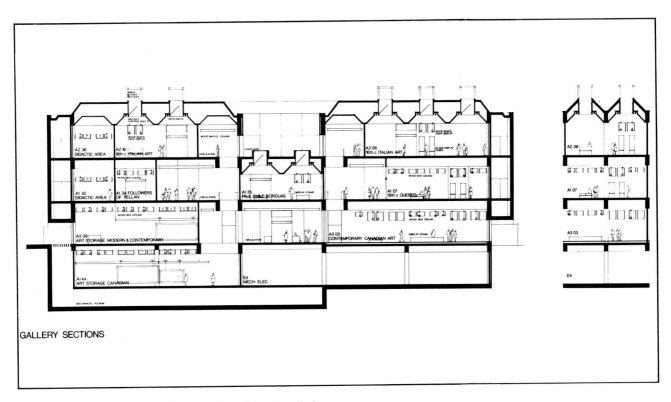

GALLERY SECTIONS

Figure 15. National Gallery, Cross-sections through galleries. WZMH proposal. (See photo of model of a typical gallery space, below right.)

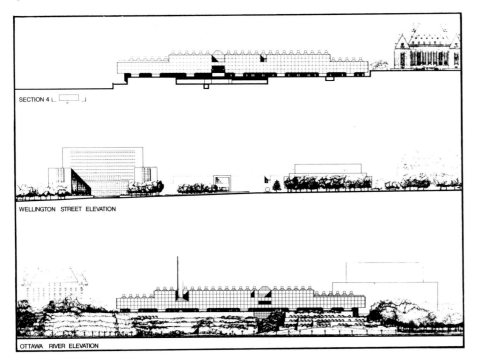

SECTION 4

WELLINGTON STREET ELEVATION

OTTAWA RIVER ELEVATION

Figure 16. National Gallery, Drawings showing principal façade on Wellington Street and Ottawa River. WZMH proposal.

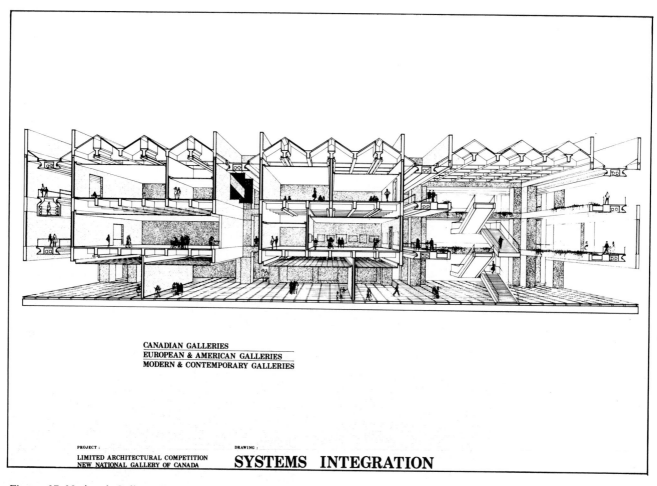

CANADIAN GALLERIES
EUROPEAN & AMERICAN GALLERIES
MODERN & CONTEMPORARY GALLERIES

PROJECT :
LIMITED ARCHITECTURAL COMPETITION
NEW NATIONAL GALLERY OF CANADA

DRAWING :

SYSTEMS INTEGRATION

Figure 17. National Gallery, Presentation panel showing a cross-section through gallery modules and connecting walkways. Parkin Architects & Planners.

Notably, the Parkin scheme was, like WZMH's proposal, the result of an in-house competition. On December 21, 1976, before the mid-February deadline, the in-house competitors gathered in the Parkin Partnership boardroom and each team made a formal presentation of its proposal. External critics had been invited to contribute an independent judgement. "Then, finally there was a hush," John Parkin recalls. "And everyone turned to me and said, 'Well?' And I said, 'If we're really concerned about standards of excellence, good architecture, and a will to win, we'll pick that scheme' . . . and I indicated the design by Bob Hopewell."

Unlike any of the other competitors' proposals, the Hopewell design standardized the relationship of galleries to circulation spaces by imposing a prominent modular form on the entire complex. Thus, rather than beginning from the "jigsaw puzzle" problems of resolv-

ing gallery dimensions with respect to the desired adjacencies, Hopewell started from an opposite, although equivalent approach. The structural unit of the building became the ordering device for the functions to be housed within. The galleries were cubes; the spaces dividing them were bridges carrying facilities: stairs, hallways, or open bridges carrying spaces, as need dictated. The intention behind the strict gridding was, as with the adjustable or "universal" galleries housed within many other competitors' proposed buildings, flexibility. John Parkin considered the pattern of movement and art display inherent in the Hopewell design as providing a "leisurely ability to go from gallery to gallery, and not be especially conscious of one's surroundings. There have to be interludes," he conceded, "but those should be peaceful interludes." *(Figures 17, 18)*

Figure 18. National Gallery, Model, Aerial view. Parkin proposal.

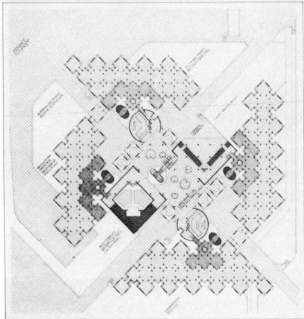

The modular organization of the proposal might also be seen as indicative of a shrewd anticipation of the jury's point of view. The Dutch architect on the jury, Professor W. G. Quist, had been considered as an exponent of modular design, and the best known examples of modular buildings, a competition scheme for Amsterdam City Hall and the Apeldoorn office complex, are the work of another Dutch architect, Herman Hertzberger. G. Stephen Vickers observed of the winning design that its appeal was its modularity. *(Figures 19, 20)*

> There was a very clear consensus that the Parkin Gallery was, like a set of child's blocks, easy to modify, especially in the event that the government did not want to spend its original budget. The possibility of building the Gallery seemed remote by the time the competition was judged, and Parkin's was the easier design to amend. It was in fact like a marriage: one was hopeful that it could change to improve.

The basic building blocks of the winning design were arranged diagonally to present a flush angled wall of mirrored glass extending from the southwest to the northeast corners of the site. The angled mirrored wall presented an oblique, reflective image to Wellington Street. *(Figure 21)*

On the river side, the modules formed a zig-zag. As a series of facets faithfully reflecting the building's modular organization, the river wall was likened by John Parkin to such masterworks of urban design as the embankments along the Thames in London or the Seine in Paris. However, because the nature of the building's structured river-side edge was unprecedented in the context of Parliament Hill, where buildings tend to stand like fortresses commanding the cliff, it was not unreservedly approved by the jury: the final report commented that the design "is not satisfactory in its treatment of the river frontage, but it is not incorrectible in this aspect. Thought should be given to the transition between the architectural structure and the river promenade." *(Figure 22)*

Figure 19. Amsterdam Town Hall Competition, Netherlands, Plan and model. Herman Hertzberger.

Right

Figure 20. National Gallery, Site plan. Parkin proposal.

Figure 21. National Gallery, Perspective rendering of principal façade. Parkin proposal.

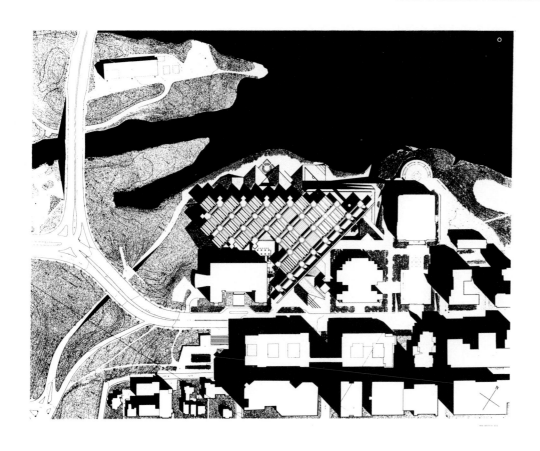

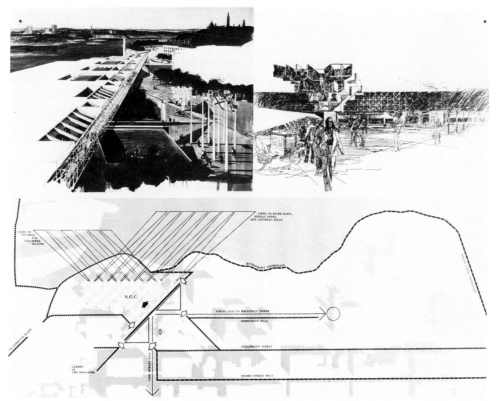

Figure 22. National Gallery, Model, River view. Parkin proposal.

But if the Parkin proposal looked uncompromising on its exterior, its underlying stripped-to-basics orderliness implied that it could at least be made smaller without costly redesign. This obviously held great appeal for the jury, whose most positive remark was that the winning design "suggests a classic solution to architectural 'delight' — subtle, unassertive and rational." The quality which distinguished it from the more subtle and unassertive "background" schemes was the astute sense of its adjustable orderliness.

What distinguished the winning scheme from the slightly different, second type of entry was that its order gave emphasis to the spirit, if not the letter, of the internal functional requirements of the programme. Architects of the second type of entry, although they also avowed that their buildings' interiors were mere backgrounds for the nation's treasures, went to greater lengths to create a distinct exterior image for the building. They marshalled the complexity of the programme by reducing the form of the building to a consistent, unmistakable shape.

The first panel of Raymond Moriyama's submission, for instance, displayed images, diagrams, and lists of words organized in an apparently free-form flow chart that made clear the architect's eagerness to pro-cede from the amorphous initial stages via a series of "dialogues" with various government departments to the "design fulfillment." Design fulfillment was illustrated by two identical images of a cup portrayed at opposite ends of the chart, subtitled "empty cup" and "full cup." This panel diagrammed the predilection, common to the second group of entries, for making a largely predetermined form "contain" the wishes of the client. *(Figure 23)*

Lacking the customary involvement of a client, however, Moriyama explained the streamlined profile of his Gallery as the outcome of wind-tunnel tests set out to determine the most energy-efficient form for the building. "When you place a heap of sand in a wind tunnel," he observed, "the form of it changes and changes until a critical point. After that, its form remains constant and it only reduces in size." Thus the building's ultimate shape was dictated by the specific forces of prevailing winds. Essentially a cube with two opposite corners eroded, it tapered down in a series of undulating contours. In the end, it looked like two earlier Moriyama buildings, the Scarborough Civic Centre and the Toronto Metro Library, both on sites with undoubtedly different wind patterns from those along Wellington Street. *(Figure 24)*

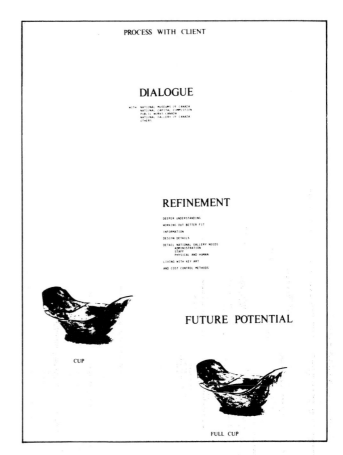

Figure 23. (Detail) National Gallery, Presentation panel showing concepts. Raymond Moriyama, Architects & Planners.

Figure 24. National Gallery, Model, Aerial view. Raymond Moriyama.

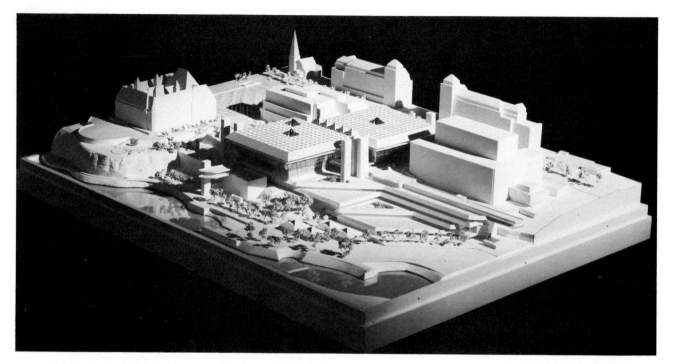

Figure 25. National Gallery, Model, Aerial view. Victor Prus, Architect & Urbanist, Montréal, with Bland Lemoyne Shine Lacroix, Architectes et Urbanistes, Montréal, with Longpré Marchand Goudreau Dobush Stewart Hein, Architects, Montreal, with Hébert Lalonde, Architectes, Montréal.

Victor Prus' design was characterized by the crystalline forms dictated by his use of an octahedral unit for the buildings' structure. The inverted eight-sided forms, with glass tilting inward to a narrower base, appeared to defy gravity, in direct contrast to neighbouring bottom-heavy Neo-classical buildings. The octahedral buildings' copper roofs, which also tilted inward, were meant to allude to the elaborate mansards of the Parliament Buildings. *(Figures 25, 26)*

The geometrical aspects of Prus' scheme were not derived (as were the triangular geometries of Pei's East Wing addition to the National Gallery in Washington) from qualities inherent in the site and the programme. The emphasis on the building's structural module did however anticipate I. M. Pei's presence on the jury.

Pei's background and interests were well known to the National Gallery entrants. His eminent career began with a job as an engineer, designing concrete mainly for defense structures. Following training as an architect at Harvard, his interest in engineering has manifested itself in the integration of pure geometrical forms and precision-designed structural systems.

"I. M. Pei is a purist," Victor Prus explains. "For him, strictly architectural qualities would be the highest criteria. In judging the competition he payed no great attention to the programme. He payed as usual very careful attention to the architectonics, to the architectural values of the building, and to the building's place in the capital city. That is his great forte."

Pei's East Wing addition to the American National Gallery (1971-1978) has in common with this second group of entries the subordination of all aspects of the building on a unified outer form. The East Wing's shape, however, was the studied result of relating a building on a triangular site (the junction of Constitution and Pennsylvania Avenues in Washington) to the Neo-classical National Gallery and its axial paths of movement. By Pei's own account:

It's very difficult to relate an asymmetrical building to a symmetrical building . . . with a very powerful axis — north, south, east and west. But to draw this line makes an isosceles triangle out of this funny-shaped polygon, and if you bisect the base, you have an axial relationship to it. So that was the most important single move, just like a chess move. Sometimes if you make the right move in playing chess, you win; sometimes you make the wrong move and everything goes wrong afterward. But that turned out to be the right move, I think. *(Figure 27)*

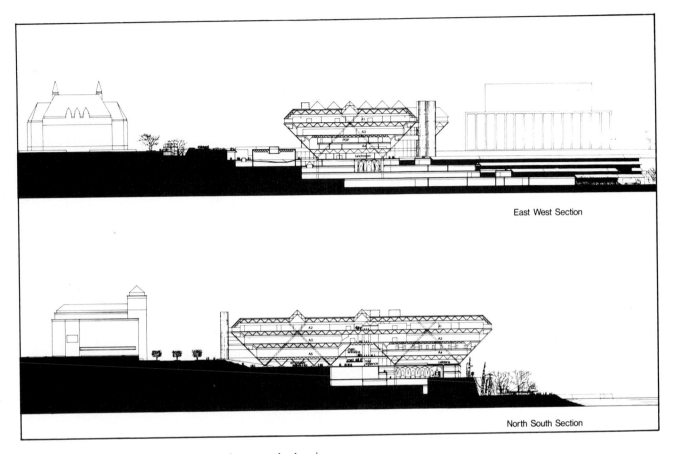

East West Section

North South Section

Figure 26. National Gallery, Presentation panel showing cross-section through the two octahedral units of the Gallery. Victor Prus team proposal.

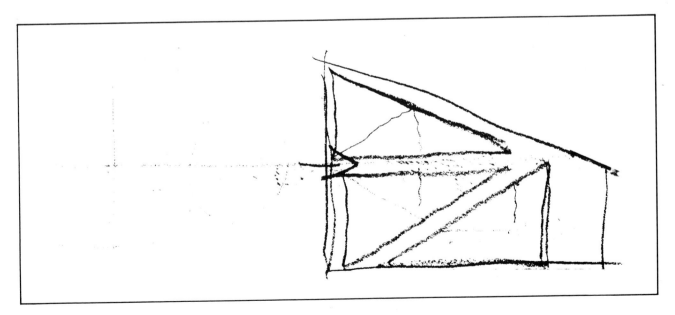

Figure 27. Sketch of the East Wing of the National Gallery in Washington, D.C. I. M. Pei.

Just as the Prus scheme concentrated on the building's structure, Arthur Erickson's team looked to the natural aspects of the site to shape the building. Wellington Street was viewed as a "checkerboard" made up of buildings (the Parliament Buildings, the Supreme Court, the proposed Federal Court, and the National Library) interspersed with open spaces. The main volume of building was located in terraces lodged in the cliff; visual connections were made to the street by a vast glazed vault, leaving open the corresponding blank space on the Wellington Street "checkerboard." Beneath the vault, a ravine-like space set with sculpture was gouged out below street level. The low horizontal terraces, like the interior sculpture garden, implied a preference for the world of nature as opposed to the street life of Parliament Hill. The ravine-like atrium's main function was to re-orient the visitor, dissociated from the urban landscape he left above, to an otherworld of nature, art treasures, and the fabricated "landscape" of the architecture itself. *(Figures 28, 29, 30)*

Figure 28. National Gallery, Model, Aerial view. Arthur Erickson Associates with David Boulva Cleve proposal.

Right
Figure 29. National Gallery, Site Plan. Arthur Erickson team proposal.
Figure 30. National Gallery, Perspective rendering of space under the glass vault of the Sculpture Court. Arthur Erickson team proposal.

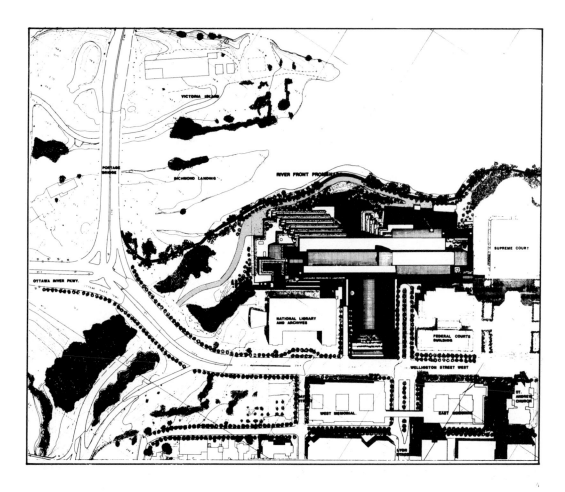

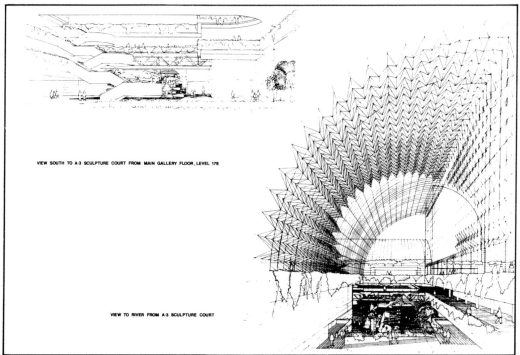

VIEW SOUTH TO A-3 SCULPTURE COURT FROM MAIN GALLERY FLOOR, LEVEL 178

VIEW TO RIVER FROM A-3 SCULPTURE COURT

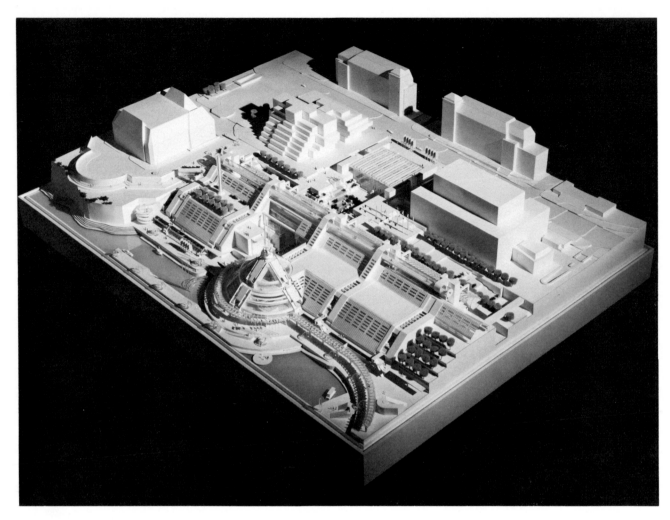

Figure 31. National Gallery, Model, Aerial view. Bregman & Hamann with C. Blake Millar.

The third group of schemes, including the work of Blake Millar, Eberhard Zeidler, and Gustavo da Roza, is characterized by a departure from the structural and geometrical concerns viewed as central to the majority of the second-stage competitors. In fact, these three design proposals have little in common with each other, apart from an apparent lack of interest in the programme minutiae, prototypical structural units, repetitive formal gestures, or the predilections of jury members. Rather than applying proven solutions to the constraints inherent in the programme and site, these architects used the competition as a means of developing social and aesthetic dimensions of their architecture.

Blake Millar, working in much the same spirit as the architects of Centre Pompidou in Paris, abandoned the tone of high seriousness that typified many of the competition proposals. His design combined the cultural functions demanded by the programme with a variety of recreational activities that were not. In the case of Millar's proposal, the colourless format required by the competition rules was especially detrimental. The building was designed to sit on a rich black-green granite base, inspired equally by existing shale formations and vegetation on the site, and the dark granite often seen around doorways of stone buildings in the area.

Above the black-green granite podium, a long, east-west glass and steel structure carried aloft the required walkway linking the building to other Parliament Hill buildings; from this look-out bridge cascaded the galleries' sloped metal rooftops. Set into the base of these metallic "slopes" was a conical steel and glass pavilion, a witty, high-tech version of the Parliamentary Library to the east. *(Figure 31)*

Figure 32. National Gallery, Perspective rendering of tour entrance and Wellington Street Reception Pavilion. Bregman & Hamann team proposal.

The building was intended to represent Millar's aesthetic, which he summarized as follows:

> In terms of contemporary and historical art, we've had a background of inspiration, if not subject matter in nature and social life. We've moved into more abstract subject matter and the use of technology. Technology has always existed in sculpture. So I used a strong natural approach combined with an overflying technical expression of steel and glass, the combination of nature and technology being a vehicle to interpret the works of man to people.

Similar to the Erickson design, a long, sunken "pavilion" extended the river bank landscape to Wellington Street, aided by an arcane mechanical system that was to combine existing storm sewers and underground currents into an indoor stream. The "pavilion," as Millar called the entrance to the Gallery, featured an immense fireplace and parasol-bedecked cafe. It was to be a place of transformation, where visitors shed the sensations and anxieties experienced on the way there, and where they simultaneously devel-

oped, as Millar calls it, "gut interest in the place." *(Figure 32)*

Blake Millar's "pavilion" typified an assumption, shared by competitors in all three groups, that visitors to the National Gallery would have to be deprogrammed on encountering the building. From many of the facades and entrances designed to introduce the public to the National Gallery, it appeared that the average visitor could be expected to feel hostility, reluctance, or boredom upon arrival at the building. Although it reflects the necessity museums face of competing for visitorship, this assumption suggests an underlying suspicion that the culture of art works is incompatible with the culture of the city at large. It was this dissociating aspect of so many of the proposals that disenchanted jurist G. Stephen Vickers. "I'm a medievalist," he explained. "I'm not really interested in seeing art removed from the environment it came from."

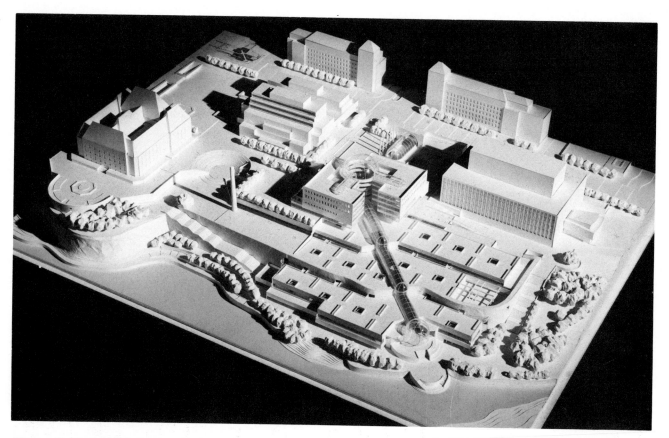

Figure 33. National Gallery, Model, Aerial view. Zeidler Partnership.

Both Eb Zeidler's and Gustavo da Roza's firms submitted proposals that flatly contradicted the assumption that art and city life are incompatible, although they were in themselves almost opposite in appearance and organization. Zeidler's team began from the premise that the National Gallery should be more than a "stage-set" for art. By elaborating on an idea close to Jean Boggs' original conception of the Gallery as an "illustrated book of the history of art," the Zeidler team discarded the option of producing a simple image for the Gallery, attempting instead to design an art complex that would revolutionize the visitor's perception of art, while adding some coherence team members felt to be lacking on the Wellington Street site.

This approach resulted in a collage of references to surrounding buildings (the river side of the main pavilion mimics the National Library next door), to buildings of the past (the central *Rotunda* and *Galleria* were modelled on Italian prototypes), and to the contours of the cliff (the galleries are lodged into the hillside in structures with both jagged and undulating forms).

As well as forcing the Gallery's integration with real and ideal urban landscapes, the design also attempted to overcome a strict linear progression from gallery to gallery in favour of a kind of art bombardment. Zeidler's Gallery housed art in terraced rooms with skylit seams that allowed visitors in one gallery to see through to other spaces and galleries simultaneously. As Zeidler team member Paul Cravit saw it, "you might see a Picasso and at the same time glimpse a Krieghoff and start to really see things." *(Figures 33, 34)*

The diagonally-oriented *Rotunda* and *Galleria* juxtaposed views into and from galleries with glimpses to the river beyond. The textbook boundaries between schools of art were subverted by this arrangement, and with them the implicit ranks of expertise dividing art experts, scholars, curators, critics, and ordinary visitors. Outside and in, the architecture freely collaged artifacts of culture, and, like any anarchist work of art, undermined the authoritative system of rules and categories that had brought its institutionalization into being. *(Figure 35)*

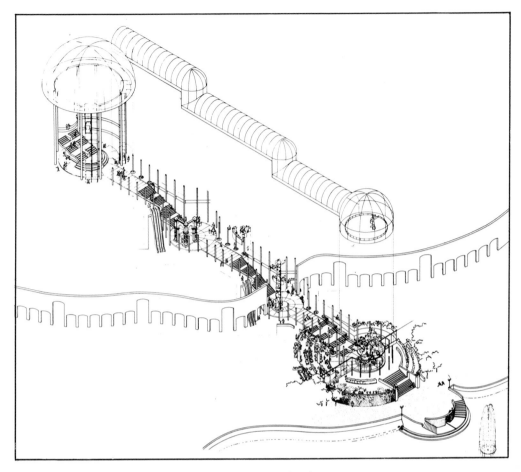

Figure 34. National Gallery, Presentation panel showing gallery and display concept. Zeidler proposal.

Figure 35. National Gallery, Presentation panel showing principal façades on Wellington Street (West Elevation) and the Ottawa River (North Elevation). Zeidler proposal.

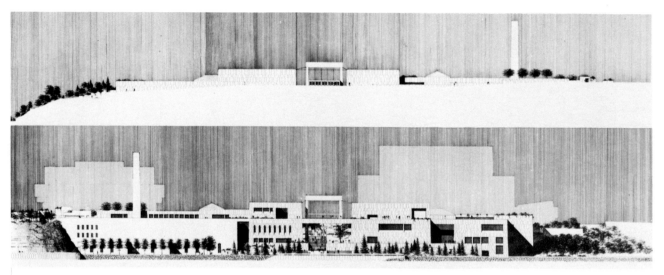

Figure 36. National Gallery, Presentation panel showing principal façades on Wellington Street and the Ottawa River. Gustavo da Roza with Number Ten Architectural Group.

Figure 37. National Gallery, Perspective rendering of the Sculpture Garden, Painters Eleven Gallery and Gallery Promenade from Scultpure Court (right). Gustavo da Roza team proposal.

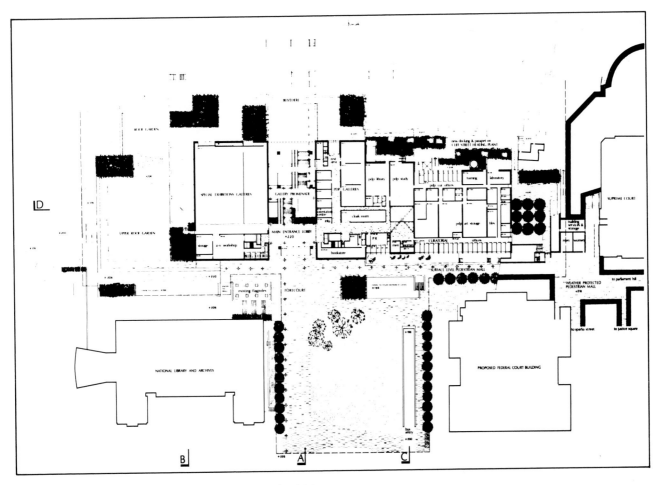

Figure 38. National Gallery, Presentation panel showing Main Entrance Level Plan. Gustavo da Roza team proposal.

Not surprisingly, the most conspicuously adventurous designs were the first eliminated by the jury. As Professor Vickers observed, "The architects on the jury made judgements on very practical concerns. The prime purpose of the building was after all to house and display the art of the National Gallery. Pei especially was disdainful of schemes with bulbous glass and irregular forms, and these were dismissed almost immediately."

In a kindred spirit to Zeidler's proposal, the first version of da Roza's design featured flamboyantly peaked copper roofs, as if to quote from the "Château style" of Parliament Hill buildings. However, the roofs were dismissed, as da Roza came to the conclusion that, "Any strong architectural statement would be too much for the hill." His second design, which he submitted to the competition, had virtually no facade on Wellington Street: the building appeared to reinterpret, rather than to mimic elements of the context.

As the visitor approached, the treed lawn rolled on as casually as if nothing had been built there. Only a bus ramp, slicing below the otherwise untouched surface, yielded a glimpse of the terraces and the stark frame of the Gallery's main public space beyond. The promenade, as this space was called, was a table-like form whose true scale only became apparent as the visitor descended a grand stair, off which the galleries were located. The long approach had the effect of a suspenseful overture, heightening the anticipation of the river view and the Gallery's collection.

From across the river, the Gallery appeared as a nascent town, its broad granite carapace forming into building blocks with windows of various dimensions and shapes. The cumulative effect, as the eye travelled over the building, was of distinct blocks grouped along open passages, and encompassed by a wall along the base of the cliff. *(Figures 36, 37, 38)*

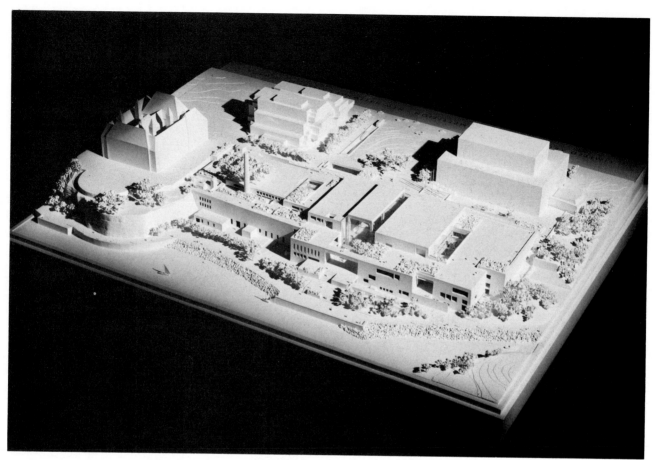

Figure 39. National Gallery, Model, Aerial view showing river side. Gustavo da Roza team proposal.

This provocative exterior image corresponded to an ingenious internal organization. The building's four floors were arranged into blocks of gallery rooms divided by courtyards and large general galleries. In marked contrast to the winning scheme, which relied on strict, modular repetition to orient the visitor, da Roza's design offered a memorable variety of room types and sizes.

In projecting the image of a city in microcosm, the da Roza Gallery is suggestive of the vital interdependence of aesthetic and cultural life. Just as much contemporary art uses form for its evocative value, as opposed to strictly simulating picturesque or abstract effects, so the da Roza design uses form to create a new but recognizable environment. *(Figure 39)*

Almost since its inception, the National Gallery has been plagued by the lack of committment to its building and budgetary requirements. Writing "Early Hardships of Canada's Great Art Collection" in 1933, T. Morris Longstreth described the various quarters of the National Gallery, setting the tone of journalism on the subject for the next half-century. The first small room to house the Royal Canadian Academy of Art was, he said, in a "building which strangers to Ottawa mistake for a stable," while its second home was in a building that also housed the Fisheries Department. According to Longstreth:

The first floor . . . was devoted to stuffed fish. A trout hatchery operated in the basement, and it was the large but completely inappropriate room on the second floor which was dedicated to incubating artists and a public appreciation of their art . . . . The caretakers were generally French. One was given to preparing her meals on the spot and with a characteristic frugality, preserved even their odors. Little boys, playing tag, rushed in and out. In winter the place, heated by a small stove, was incredibly cold. In summer, without ventilation, it was just as incredibly hot. All in all, it required considerable stamina even to be a visitor. For a director it was poisonous.

Longstreth applauded the Gallery's 1910 move into a wing of the Victoria Museum: "At last the Director could move about in an atmosphere free of frying onions, free of the damp of the fish-hatchery and the periodic R.C.A. disorders, and observe his treasures." He called it "the long-suffering, if not despised, National Gallery," a view which seemed even more applicable in the wake of the 1977 competition than in Longstreth's day.

In 1954, the first competition was held to produce a design for a National Gallery building. In anticipation of new quarters, the Gallery's staff and collections moved into the newly constructed Lorne Building, an eight-storey office building at the corner of Elgin and Slater Streets. Built for civil service workers, it was supposed to provide a temporary haven for the nation's art while the competition winning scheme was built on nearby Cartier Square. Soon after the Gallery's "temporary" move into the Lorne Building, the government announced it could not justify expenditure on a new Gallery building. Subsequently, the high humidity levels required to prevent deterioration of art works have caused the Lorne Building to itself deteriorate. Leaks, cold drafts, and frost create an intolerable environment inside, and the exterior cladding has also been damaged by the extreme differential between indoor and outdoor temperature and humidity levels. The building's notoriously poor condition has both interfered with installations and deterred potential Gallery visitors. *(Figure 40)*

The public has grown increasingly indifferent to the prospect of viewing the four per cent of the collection that will fit onto the cramped and condensation-ridden walls of the National Gallery, and attendance has declined steadily since the early Seventies. The Federal Government, meanwhile, has paid for its 1959 "economy" by pouring over $6 million into essential repairs to an office building that originally cost $5.2 million.

Secretary of State John Roberts' 1977 announcement, immediately following the second competition, that "There is no automatic committment to proceed," and that construction "would have to be reviewed in the light of current fiscal restraints" heralded a five-year long postponement of plans for a National Gallery building.

During those five years, the Department of Public Works has quietly pursued a number of options for a scaled-down National Gallery. One of the options considered was, as Professor Vickers had foreseen, an amended version of the Parkin team's competition-winning proposal, scaled down not because it was over-

Figure 40. National Gallery of Canada, The Lorne Building, Ottawa.

sized, but because of the inflation of its costs over time. By 1980, the year of the Gallery's Centennial, and the original target date for construction of Parkin's design, no progress had been made. Director H'sio Yen-Shih, Jean Boggs' successor, resigned.

The sense that nothing might come of their efforts haunted some competitors throughout both stages of the work. Ronald Dick recalled that, despite the unavoidable competition euphoria that comes in the final moments of seeing the overtime schedule materialize in a pristine, professionally-made model, he worried frequently about the "lack of good faith on the part of the sponsor. Yes, it was going to go ahead. Everybody knew it was going to go ahead. But in the back of our minds we knew it was a political football. We've run into these things before. You go in and nothing ever happens."

The skepticism and bitterness felt by many competitors in the five years following the competition was shared by those involved in the organization of the contest. Having approved the programme Desbarats later concluded:

> Most of the entries could have gone on to working drawings. In a sense (the competitors) did more work than was necessary to judge them . . . . The solutions were good but not out of the ordinary. They showed that Canadian architecture had reached a level of maturity which was quite interesting but not transcendental . . . . There was a strange levelling out of individuality in the schemes. Several had the same themes. It's a bit of a joke, but we were almost unable to guess who had done which. We could not recognize individual styles. We tended to cross them . . . . Ten to twelve years ago I think I could have guessed seven out of ten. This time I could recognize only one.

The Gallery's project leader for the competition, Gyde Shepherd, observed after the 1977 competition was over:

> The competition process seems to have a promise of a final moment of realization at the end. It's an illusion . . . . The public assumes that whenever the government does anything, it's done to camouflage something, to neutralize rather than expedite. People suspect institutions. There's a nervousness about the country that doesn't have anything to do with understanding history or understanding symbols or creating new ones. But people have a very real need to see pictures. There has to be a single story told somewhere.

The use of public money to promote the nation's fine arts has a long, vexed history in Canada. On the Gallery's side, curators and administrators have maintained that a dollar value cannot be assigned to culture. In an interview with Sandra Peredo, Dr. Shih contended that, "Artists have special visions, and whether we paid $300, $3000, or $3 million shouldn't determine what is shown in a national gallery . . . . [The price of works of art] is not public because in this very commercial work people think price equates with quality."

Nevertheless, the relegation of the National Gallery to Federal Government control necessarily makes the issue of value economic as well as aesthetic. When Parliament received a request from the National Gallery in 1966 to spend $885,000 on four paintings (two by Chardin, one by Simone Martini, and one by Rubens) from the Lichtenstein collection, Ross Thatcher delivered a speech which typified the conflict: "What does the expenditure of $885,000 mean in terms of farming? I would point out that it represents about 650,000 bushels of wheat, the total output of approximately 125 prairie farmers for a year. It represents about 6,000 steers, I suppose — grain-fed ones at that."

The assignment of dollar values to art, apparently inevitable in this "very commercial world," has contributed to the differences between architects and artists, driving them into endorsement or rejection of commercial interests. In a 1961 speech, "Relationships: Art in Architecture," John Parkin proposed that, "Historically, the last century has seen the architect grow closer to the engineer, and grow correspondingly more distant from the artist. While the artist withdrew to his studio, the architect became more "practical"; as the architect became the product of logic, painting and sculpture isolated themselves in the field of metaphysics."

Like Parkin, I. M. Pei associates the alienation of art from architecture to the ascendance of technology. He has said that "the days are gone when one man could be both artist and architect. The technological complexity of modern life alone would inhibit Renaissance man." While both men are renowned for their interest in engineering and their reliance on technical solutions in their architecture (Parkin's firm was amongst the first in Canada to adopt the name "architects and engineers" and he holds honorary doctoral degrees in Science and Engineering), Parkin's attitude to the rift between art and architecture is more extreme than Pei's. Parkin has expressed the view that "new social . . . and economic forces have tended to restrict the experimentation and application of art in architecture." Pei, by contrast, recently collaborated with artists Kenneth Noland and Dan Flavin on the design of the Arts and Media Building at M.I.T.

Flavin was reported in a 1980 interview with Pei to be integrating his fluorescent tube sculpture with the building's lighting system, and Noland was said to be participating in design of the building's structural joints. In Pei's words, "The artist's work will not be an individual work of art standing in space or hung on a wall. It will be part of the building, a permanent part of the environment."

Soon after John Roberts' announcement concerning the postponement of the National Gallery's construction, Bob Hopewell left the Parkin Partnership to work as a freelance designer for a number of firms, later becoming a partner of the WZMH Partnership. Holding to the lessons learned thirty years earlier at Harvard, John Parkin maintains his view that design is one component of architecture among many others. "The legal responsibility rests with me," he claims. "Those people [the design architects] come and go. They all work for every one of us. They move from office to office. The work of the architect is not that of the journalist but of the editor and publisher.''

The social crusade of the European Modernists, seen from an albeit very altered Canadian perspective, has remained an important factor in Parkin's architectural outlook. In a 1978 speech entitled "Château and Substance," Parkin proposed, "If we have no great cities in the sense that Venice or Paris or Rome are great, it is because such cities were created by the fiat of despots. Whatever their glories, they are not apt to be duplicated within the framework of a Parliamentary democracy and a free-enterprise economy."

John Parkin has praised I. M. Pei as "a great architect, artistic and intellectual. He understands the structures of power." Parkin, too understands the structures of Canadian power, and his views on the respective roles of architects, artists, engineers, and clients touch on the most fundamental issue for mainstream architecture. Having risen to prominence on the wave of post-War economic expansion, indeed having advanced many of the same values as their expansion-oriented clientele, what will the large multi-disciplinary practices become with the onset of declining economic growth and public skepticism about institutional development?

After the competition, Guy Desbarats observed that "concrete symbols of pride and achievement are things our government has not been anxious to create."

What this admission indicates is that, in the end, the National Gallery competition was not so much a contest for the best design, but a rationalization for why design, urban and architectural, has grown to be less and less the preoccupation underlying mainstream architecture. For in its identification with the structures of power, the architectural establishment is now coming to terms with the adjustments in those structures. To advance, the mainstream will need to alter its course to explore the new avenues that are the subject of the chapters which follow.

As this book went to press in 1982, Prime Minister Pierre Trudeau and Communications Minister Francis Fox announced that the Federal Government has given a firm go-ahead to the construction of new buildings for both the National Gallery and the National Museum of Man. Dr. Jean Sutherland Boggs has left her post as Director of the Philadelphia Museum of Art to become the president of a special public corporation which will choose architects, sites, and ultimately, designs for both buildings, in consultation with the National Museums Corporation, the National Capital Commission and the directors of both museums. In the press releases issued on February 18, 1982, no mention was made of the Department of Public Works or its 1976 competition.

III   The Will to Conserve

By the time the oil crisis struck in 1973, concern for the environment had been growing in Canada as elsewhere. Pollution Probe had been founded in 1969 to monitor environmental and energy issues. In that same year, Ontario had limited the use of DDT to bat and mouse control, and the International Joint Commission, having studied the pollution in the lower Great Lakes, had advised the Canadian and U.S. governments to immediately reduce the use of phosphates to a minimum practical level. In Halifax, Toronto and Vancouver (as in New Orleans, New York and San Francisco) community groups battled against the destruction of inner city neighbourhoods and their replacement by anonymous, isolated highrises or, even worse, by the superhighways required to carry greater numbers of people between their suburban houses and downtown commercial cores.

But the oil crisis marked a real turning point. Although in Canada the crisis was at first more a matter of anxious anticipation than of real scarcity, it sparked a genuine change in attitudes towards both the natural and built environment. In the course of a post-1973 decline in the western world's economic health, notions of unlimited growth and technological progress, notions epitomized by Expo, were called into question. Where before there had been a handful of acutely perceptive critics — Jane Jacob's *The Death and Life of Great American Cities* was published in 1961, Rachel Carson's *Silent Spring*, in 1963 — and but a few, isolated, protesting citizens fearful of losing their homes and neighbourhoods, there was suddenly a whole society faced with a threat to its prosperous way of life.

Changes in Canada's political climate were also caused by a general perception that the underlying structure of Canadian society was gradually beginning to shift. A similar perception in the United States gave rise to an intellectual movement labelled Neo-Conservatism. Espousing the values of continuity and hierarchy, this U.S. movement struck a responsive chord in Canada.

Not simply a reactionary force, the new conservatism has provided the basis for a new and progressive way of looking at the environment. It has produced a number of bold and important projects which have sought to save key neighbourhoods of our cities from obscurity or destruction.

The Promenade, Halifax

When the City of Halifax proposed a cross-town expressway alongside its waterfront in the late sixties, it did so because here, it seemed, lay the path of least resistance and, hopefully, the makings of a picturesque drive. Because the expressway would have destroyed the run-down but historic, waterfront district, citizen opposition arose in response to the idea. A group calling itself the "Committee of Concern and the Heritage Trust of Nova Scotia," and including Halifax architect Allen Duffus, made a formal submission to City Council, outlining the value of the waterfront district.

The submission argued that restoration of existing buildings could be carried out without overwhelming difficulty, and it cited as precedents projects such as Bastion Square in Victoria and Old Montreal. New uses for the waterfront were proposed, many of them related to existing structures and uses. A public marina was suggested as the most obvious and simplest function with provision for indigenous maritime industries, like yacht supply and customs brokerage, as well as for tourist-related businesses. "Imaginatively restored and developed," suggested the Heritage Trust, "this complex could provide Halifax with both a reflection of its early maritime heritage and a productive enterprise in a renewed city."

The Heritage Trust appealed directly to the public with an advertisement placed in the *Halifax/Herald Mail Star.* "These buildings," explained the ad, "are an historic heritage of the citizens of Halifax and the people of Canada." The ad asked citizens to sign their names to a form which said: "Please reconsider your decision to demolish the historic waterfront buildings," and to mail it to City Hall. "The response," Allan Duffus recalls, "was unbelievable. The Mayor and City Councillors were flooded with mail and telephone calls."

Responding to public interest — the Mayor received more letters in favour of retaining the waterfront buildings than he had on any other single civic issue — City Council rescinded its earlier decision to demolish the historic buildings, and called for proposals to develop the area.

A little less than four and one-half acres in size, the historic district was one of the last remnants of Halifax's early and prosperous beginnings. Located at the City's southeastern waterfront edge, the small pocket of nineteenth-century, brick, stone and wood buildings had as neighbours the multi-block, multi-tower Scotia Square to the west, and bank towers and a new courthouse building to the south.

Two proposals were received. "Harborside 1850," submitted by Californian Robert Abbott, proposed, amongst other features, a convention centre and a lighthouse. Abbott's plan was rejected in favour of a less flamboyant proposal by Halifax developer John Fiske, who had hired Allen Duffus' architectural firm, Duffus Romans Kundzins Rounsefell, to work out the design.

The overall intent of the Duffus Romans Kundzins Rounsefell plan was to enhance the existing buildings and to knit the area together by means of a pedestrian route which would run from the waterfront westward towards Scotia Square, linking the three main segments of the historic area. The first segment was a group of seven early warehouse buildings on the water's edge. The second was a block, on the east side of Granville Street, of commercial buildings (1859-63) destined to contain "The Promenade." And the third was a block of buildings on the west side of Granville Street, planned for redevelopment as a hotel. This block was to be connected to the Scotia Square development by a pedestrian walkway. *(Figures 41, 42)*

Duffus offered a "restoration philosophy" as the basis for his firm's design. The nineteenth-century identity of the buildings would be conserved and serviced to meet modern-day needs, while the nineteenth-century character of the open spaces would be maintained and enhanced by the use of street furniture, paving and landscaping. The whole area was to be developed as a "pedestrian precinct," with automobile access limited to service vehicles; and as an "historic precinct," a self-contained community that would not only attract visitors and tourists but also would be a pleasant place to live and work. Duffus' proposal was able to go ahead when the Nova Scotia College of Art and Design and Parks Canada agreed to rent space in the revitalized district. The College was especially supportive, committing itself as a tenant in the project for the next thirty-four years.

The Halifax waterfront restoration was completed in 1981. It can be best understood, like most architectural projects, by touring the area on foot. Starting at the water's edge, it soon becomes apparent that the restoration of the waterfront warehouses and the addition of the three new ones has been largely but not entirely successful. The buildings comprising this area's extraordinary architectural heritage — the Privateer's Warehouse (c.1810), where goods "legally" pirated from enemy ships were stored until they could be sold at public auction, and the Collins Bank and Warehouse (1825), the first private bank in Nova Scotia — have

Figure 41. Outdoor square on Halifax harbour.

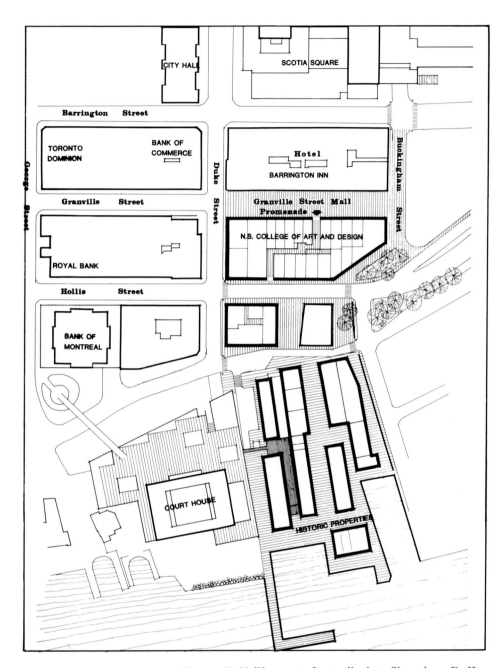

Figure 42. Halifax waterfront district, Site plan. Duffus Romans Kundzins Rounsefell, Architects.

been carefully rehabilitated. Their nineteenth-century seaside flavour remains intact.

It is in the addition of the new buildings, and in the use of the spaces between buildings to create two new areas, that this segment of the Halifax restoration has had mixed results. The first of these new areas is an outdoor square fashioned from a previously-unused space between two parallel warehouses. The second is an entirely new indoor mall which is defined on one side by an old warehouse and on the other by a new row of shops.

The outdoor square is a vibrant place. With sound bouncing off stone walls and salt in the air, it offers views of the harbour and casually-arranged seating places.

Figure 43. Indoor mall, Halifax harbour. Duffus Romans Kundzins Rounsefell, Architects.

The indoor mall, on the other hand, is somewhat anonymous in character. Although its spaciousness, abundant natural light and exposed, barn-like structure make it an attractive place, the *place*, by and large, could be anywhere. Entry is gained only by the doors at either end and, once inside, views to the surrounding area and particularly to the harbour are severed. The inward-looking character of the mall inevitably has had an effect on the adjacent harbourfront land, where no special provision has been made, either for walking or sitting, for visitors to the water's edge. *(Figure 43)*

Uphill and inland from the waterfront warehouses is Granville Street, historically one of the most important commercial streets of Halifax. A great fire swept through the street in 1859 and, according to a contemporary account in the *London Illustrated News*, "Houses and stores, wooden, brick, and stone alike, fed the flames until . . . sixty of the finest buildings in Halifax . . . were destroyed." Following the fire, one of Canada's largest architecture firms, William Thomas and Sons, was chosen to redesign what the London paper would later term "the Haligonian's Paradise":

Granville Street.

The result was an energetic row of four-storey buildings. At street level, elegant glass and iron storefronts enticed those passing by with luxurious displays. Above, facades of multicoloured brick and stone, with windows capped by round and pointed arches, made reference to Venetian Gothic, Romanesque, and Italian Renaissance architecture. Characteristic of Thomas' style, as also evidenced in the Don Jail in Toronto, sculptured masks — some comical, others highly serious — look out from their positions atop many of the block's windows. *(Figures 44, 45)*

By clearing out the block's former service area, a two-level promenade running parallel to Granville and Hollis Streets was created. Logically called "The Promenade," its two levels are enclosed by a new roof of heavy timbers interspersed with skylights. Two former shops, one on Granville, the other on Hollis, have been used to provide entrances and lobbys to The Promenade, creating a graceful transition between the old street and the new promenade.

Figures 44,45. The eastern side of Granville Street, Halifax. Thomas & Sons, Original Architects; Duffus Romans Kundzins Rounsefell, Restoration.

Figure 46. A former Granville Street shop made into a vestibule of The Promenade, Halifax. Duffus Romans Kundzins Rounsefell, Architects.

The Granville Street entrance is marked by a canvas canopy and leads to a clean, white vestibule well-lit by its glass front to the street. To the left is a small plaque reading "The Nova Scotia College of Art and Design," and a locked door, slim evidence of the presence of the College in the warehouse space above the stores. From this vestibule, one continues towards The Promenade itself, through a doorway flanked by Corinthian columns and capped by a Moorish-style arch. *(Figure 46)*

Through the arch and another smaller vestibule, perpendicular to the visitor's line of entry, is the upper, skylit level of The Promenade. Entry from Hollis Street, on the other side of the block, brings one into The Promenade's lower, crypt-like level. Upper and lower levels merge in a provocative, multi-levelled space, a powerful focus for The Promenade and therefore the whole carefully-rehabilitated waterfront district of Halifax.

Figure 47. The Promenade, Halifax. Restored cast-iron columns with gold-painted capitals.

Figure 48. The Promenade, Halifax, Multi-levelled central space. Duffus Romans Kundzins Rounsefell, Architects.

Figure 49. Skylights and carefully placed windows provide unusual views out of The Promenade.

From this central space, one can see back out through the stores on both levels to the street. The backs of the stores have been replaced by glass, and cast-iron Corinthian columns have been retained, their shafts painted black and capitals gold. Skylights above the upper level reveal the backs of the Hollis Street buildings rising above, enticing a comparison between identical windows, some now inside, some still outside. *(Figures 47, 48, 49)*

The block on the western side of Granville Street, the final third of the initial master plan, has been partially restored, but mostly rebuilt as Barrington Place Inn, by the architects Page and Steele. It is now a 200-room hotel with stores on the lower levels. The renovation of this block is in some ways clever, but it is more successful on the outside than it is on the inside.

Although the facades of this four storey block were, where possible, retained, the inside of the block was completely gutted and replaced by a new concrete structure and brand new interior. Interestingly enough, because of the extent of the work on the interior, the facades had to be disassembled stone-by-stone, numbered and replaced onto the face of the "new building" in the same painstaking manner.

A new, fifth storey was added to the block in the form of a steeply-pitched mansard roof set back from the face of the restored facades. It is an addition which is skillful and sensitive to the proportions and feel of the existing exterior. Ultimately, however, this carefully renovated exterior gives way to a modern, "international" hotel interior which lacks the interest and regional character of The Promenade across the street.

Sussex Drive Redevelopment, Ottawa

Like The Promenade, the Sussex Drive Redevelopment project in Ottawa reflects a recent trend towards re-use of what were yesterday's service spaces, hidden from view in the middle of buildings or whole blocks. The project was born in 1961 when the National Capital Commission (N.C.C.) received Cabinet approval to acquire and preserve four blocks of heritage commercial buildings (1850-1870) along Sussex Drive. The intent at the time was simply to preserve the buildings from demolition and in 1964 the Sussex Drive facades were cleaned, repaired and painted.

By 1970, the plans of the N.C.C. for the area had gone beyond that of mere preservation, perhaps due in part to the appointment of Arthur Capling as Chief Architect. In hope of creating an alternative to the formal and ceremonial nature of Sussex Drive, which is the main boulevard leading from Parliament Hill to the prime minister's residence, the governor-general's residence, Rideau Hall, and Rockcliffe Park, the N.C.C. embarked on a programme of restoring the internal courts of the four blocks along Sussex Drive which it owned. Up until this time, these spaces were used for deliveries, storage and parking. *(Figure 50)*

Figure 50. Sussex Drive Redevelopment project, Ottawa, Site plan. From right to left: Clarendon Court, York Court, Place Jeanne d'Arc, Tin House Court. National Capital Commission, Arthur Capling, Chief Architect.

Partially completed by 1979, the idiosyncratic and picturesque nature of these former service spaces is emphasized by the casual placement of fountains, trees, benches, and sculpture against the two- to four-storey brick and stone nineteenth-century buildings. Art galleries, restaurants and shops open onto the courts, while apartments and offices look down from the upper stories. *(Figures 51, 52)*

If there is a fault with the project, it is in the failure to relate the courts to Ottawa's streets. As a result, the spaces are not as heavily used or as dynamic as they might be. The courts are often entered via unmarked passages and the areas themselves are isolated not only from the streets but also from each other. They seem more like well-cared-for private spaces than like extensions of the public realm. *(Figure 53)*

The Tin House Court exemplifies this problem. This court takes its name from an elaborate house facade, made partially out of tin, which was salvaged before the rest of the house was demolished, and later hung on one of the interior court walls as "art." It is a small gesture, probably meant as a metaphor for preservation. However, it imparts an unreal character to the court, pointing out the especially fragile and delicate nature of these nineteenth-century blocks, turned partially but not entirely inside out. *(Figure 54)*

Figures 51, 52. Sussex Drive Redevelopment project, Ottawa. Views into the courts. Arthur Capling, Chief Architect.

Figure 56. York Quay Centre, Harbourfront, Toronto, with its outdoor cafe over the water.

Figure 57. A passage along the water's edge.

The period from 1972 to 1980 has been marked by a steady but gentle upgrading of the site, so as to make it more attractive and accessible to the public. This was done, primarily, by introducing community events and park-like elements into what quite purposefully remained an intriguing, semi-industrial waterfront landscape.

Among the most important park-like elements introduced was Harbourfront Passage, a paved route through and around the area, mostly along the water's edge, marked by planters, benches, flags, and information kiosks at important points. On the York Quay, the Direct Winters Building (formerly the warehouse and offices of a trucking company) was cleaned-up and renovated to include a theatre, an art gallery, a string of artist's studios adjacent to but set down from an interior public walkway, and a café leading onto an outdoor deck overlooking Lake Ontario. Across the street, another warehouse provides a home for a Sunday flea market during the winter months. Until recently, in warmer months, the market moved out and under the brightly-painted steel skeleton of a foundry building, erected in 1917 for the purpose of building freighters as part of the War effort. *(Figures 56, 57, 58)*

During this period of gradual change, Harbourfront has gained steadily in popularity, drawing 15,000 visitors in 1974, and 1.5 million in 1980. The future of Harbourfront, however, lies not only in the increasing number of visitors expected, but in the number of *residents* who, it is hoped by those involved, will make the area their home in the years ahead.

Figure 58. Harbourfront, the steel skeleton which formerly housed the Sunday flea market in summer months has now been demolished.

This fundamental shift in planning philosophy was proposed as part of the larger "Harbourfront Development Framework," prepared by the firm of Coombes Kirkland Berridge, for the Harbourfront Corporation in 1978. In contrast to the gentle upgrading of the site which preceeded it, this "guide to the physical future of the site" proposes a major development, entailing demolition, renovation and new construction, to create an overall system of parks, streets, services and buildings. Ambitiously hoping to attract $200 million in private investment to the site, and with a time frame of seven years for implementation (1981-1987), the proposal was approved in June 1980. At that time the owner of the site, the federal government, committed $27.5 million to help build the required infrastructure of roads, sewers and services. *(Figure 59)*

The need for such large-scale development along the water's edge was questioned by a number of people who wondered how the federal government could approve over 750,000 square metres (approximately eight million square feet) of new construction for an area originally scheduled to become a park. John Clarry, Chairman of the Metro Board of Trade's Harbourfront Committee, was among those who spoke out

publicly against the development. He argued that its scale was inappropriate, and that the number of residents proposed for the area (10,000) was *at least* 5,000 too many. "People don't appreciate the kind and size of development that is being planned," he said. "This is supposed to be a parkland for the people of Metro [Toronto] . . . ."

The *Globe and Mail*, in a May 19, 1980 editorial entitled "Parkland Invaders," criticized the Harbourfront Corporation and Toronto City Hall for proposing to "push the public back behind private and public housing and commercial buildings."

Much of this concern is justified. Inevitably, views of the water from Queen's Quay will be blocked by the new construction. In an attempt to connect one end of the site with the other, a new road will be introduced along the length of the site which will bridge, divide and inexorably alter two of the existing "slips," or inlets between the quays. The largest single occupant of the site, Maple Leaf Mills Ltd., which spans two separate quays which are generally termed one, is being eliminated entirely, despite the fact that its grain elevators on the site were listed by the Toronto Historical Board for "architectural," "historical," and "contextual"

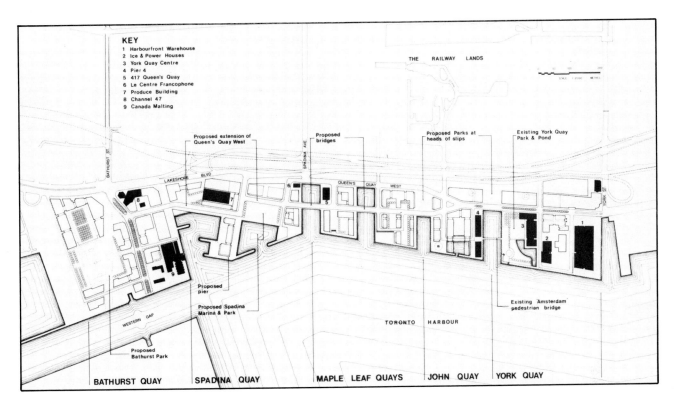

KEY
1 Harbourfront Warehouse
2 Ice & Power Houses
3 York Quay Centre
4 Pier 4
5 417 Queen's Quay
6 Le Centre Francophone
7 Produce Building
8 Channel 47
9 Canada Malting

THE RAILWAY LANDS

Proposed extension of Queen's Quay West

Proposed bridges

Proposed Parks at heads of slips

Existing York Quay Park & Pond

LAKESHORE BLVD

QUEEN'S QUAY WEST

SPADINA AVE

BATHURST ST

YORK ST

Proposed pier

Proposed Spadina Marina & Park

Existing Amsterdam pedestrian bridge

WESTERN GAP

TORONTO HARBOUR

Proposed Bathurst Park

BATHURST QUAY | SPADINA QUAY | MAPLE LEAF QUAYS | JOHN QUAY | YORK QUAY

Figure 59. Harbourfront Development Framework, 1978 plan, Toronto. Coombes Kirkland Berridge, Urban Design.

reasons. The steel skeleton of the former foundry building on the Spadina Quay, previously the home of the Sunday flea market during warmer months, has now been demolished.

On the other hand, many of the best of the existing waterfront buildings will be retained and revitalized in the new development. The eight-storey Terminal Warehouse, a great 90,000-square-metre (approximately million-square-foot) hulk of a building which was one of Canada's early poured-in-place concrete structures, is being renovated by the Zeidler Roberts Partnership. When completed it will contain a mix of retail activities situated on the ground floors around a number of atria, a 450-seat dance auditorium on the third floor, offices in the middle levels and penthouse condominiums built on the roof.

The York Quay Centre will remain, along with a number of other buildings of architectural and historical interest, such as Le Centre Francophone and the Produce Building. Canada Malting, the area's second largest occupant, will continue its operations on Bathurst Quay at the western edge of the site. Its grain elevator, also listed by the Toronto Historical Board, will remain as well. *(Figures 60, 61)*

The proposed buildings will be arranged so as to create public courtyards and passages between them, maximizing views and actual access to the water's edge. However, in order to keep as much of the land as possible accessible to the public, three-storey housing units have been ruled out in favour of apartment buildings six-storeys and up.

The federal government's original concept of the "waterfront park," has never really been defined (or designed), and thus has always been too vague to garner much support. The Harbourfront Corporation, for instance, dismisses the "waterfront park" concept as "an idea . . . that the ninety-one acres stretching from York Street to Bathurst could simply be levelled and made into a vast green lawn."

Many of Toronto's citizens, and certainly many of its landscape architects, will always be puzzled over the suggestion that a park, must, by necessity, be a "vast green lawn." This having been said, the new "Harbourfront Development Framework" can be credited with combining an overall respect for the existing Harbourfront buildings, with a desire to use old and new buildings together to create and define a series of public spaces and promenades along the water's edge.

The firm of Coombes Kirkland Berridge has attempted to make the development as "un-project-like" as possible. Roads — in architect Michael Kirkland's words, "the virtual stuff of public space" — have been made smaller in size but more numerous. Development of all five quays will not be done at once, but in phases quay-by-quay, and probably by different architects. Whether the "sub-area," or quay-by-quay developments live up to the promise of the area in general and the Framework in particular, is something around which the historical and future character of Harbourfront will revolve.

Figures 60,61. Harbourfront, Queen's Quay Terminal. Exterior and interior renderings of the proposed renovation by Zeidler Roberts Partnership, Architects.

Granville Island, Vancouver

Three years after it had spent somewhere between $80 and $100 million on the purchase of 36.8 hectares (91 acres) of Toronto's waterfront, the federal government made a similar but smaller purchase of $11 million of leases on Granville Island, a 15.4 hectare (38-acre) industrial peninsula several minutes drive from downtown Vancouver. Unlike Harbourfront, this purchase was not part of an election campaign, but rather in response to a specially-commissioned redevelopment study done of the site, by the Vancouver firm of Thompson Berwick Pratt and Partners. The Granville Island project was also unlike Harbourfront in that the intent for the area was established at the outset.

As recommended in the study, a five-member commission was appointed to manage development of the site. Named the Granville Island Trust, the commission made the decision to retain much of the existing industry on the site prior to hiring Norman Hotson Architects to design a master plan for the "island." *(Figure 62)*

Figure 62. Granville Island, Vancouver, Master plan. Norman Hotson Architects.

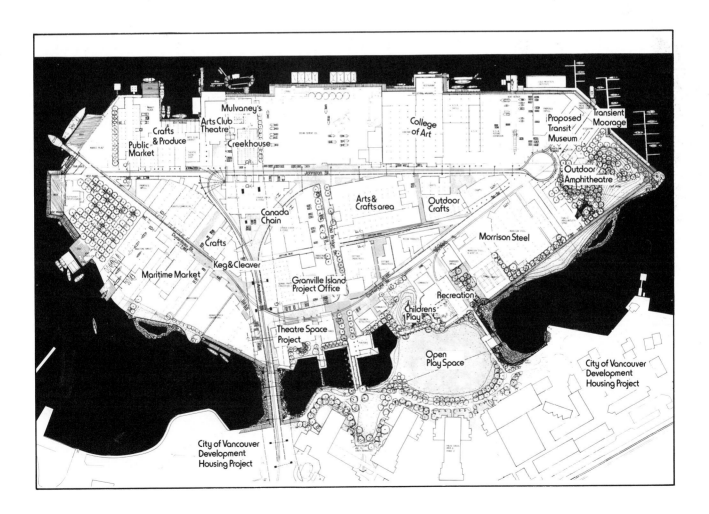

Architect Norman Hotson was sympathetic to the commission's goal of upgrading the existing industrial buildings and of infilling between and around these buildings so as to create facilities which would augment but not supercede the daily manufacturing of concrete and metal products on the site. "We wanted to create a public amenity," explains Hotson, "not a park. . . . In today's cities, all land uses are segregated. Our idea was to return to the original roots of settlement, to create something more village-like where all land uses are in one place."

Prefiguring Toronto's Harbourfront Development Framework of 1978, no attempt was made to separate cars and pedestrians in the 1977 Granville Island master plan. Unfortunately for cars, but perhaps fortunately for pedestrians, the existing road network on the island was, and remains, as confusing and convoluted as it could possibly be. There are still no sidewalks, permitting people to use the streets for strolling. As a result, cars crawl about the island at a speed roughly equivalent to that of the people walking alongside. *(Figures 63, 64)*

Figures 63,64. Granville Island, an atmosphere of "randomness, curiosity, delight and surprise."

In fact, the easy-going and seemingly idiosyncratic development of the site, whereby the urban designers hoped to create an atmosphere of "randomness, curiosity, delight and surprise," imparts an air of joy. A system of plain timber posts runs along the street and through the buildings themselves, supporting colourful awnings, light fixtures and other street furnishings. The public market is housed in a warehouse renovated by the Hotson firm. Pulleys still dangle from the ceiling and a fat red pipe, supported by timber posts, snakes in and out of the building, suggesting alignment for the market stalls and lights. *(Figures 65,66,67)*

The impact of the island's simple warehouse and industrial facades has been strengthened by the judicious use of strong colour, striped awnings, and the careful placement of lighting fixtures. A number of new buildings pick up this casual theme of colourful, corrugated metal buildings with eclectic openings and fittings. New and old buildings work remarkably well with each other to impart an easy-going, accommodating and spirited character to Granville Island. *(Figures 68, 69)*

Figures 65, 66, 67. The Granville Island Public Market, interior and exterior views. Norman Hotson, Architect.

Figure 68, 69. Granville Island, The work of Barbara Dalrymple (above) and Norman Hotson (below). Simple warehouse facades, strong colours and eclectic openings and fittings are characteristic of the ''island'' as a whole.

Corridart and the 1976 Olympics, Montreal

More cerebral, much more short-lived and probably no less fun than Granville Island, Montreal's Corridart was a street festival-*cum*-urban documentary that was to have been part of the 1976 Olympics. It lasted only a week because Montreal's Mayor, Jean Drapeau, had it ripped down in the middle of the night . . . but that's getting ahead of the story.

Because it hoped that the 1976 Olympic Games would be more than just an athletic celebration, the Organizing Committee for the '76 Games (COJO) established an "Arts and Culture Programme." As part of that programme, Montreal architect Melvin Charney was hired to design, organize and coordinate his concept of an 8.4 kilometre-long (5.5 mile-long) "museum in the street."

Sherbrooke Street was the natural place for such an event. It has a long history as one of Montreal's premier boulevards, and the Olympic Park was located on its eastern end. The idea was to make Sherbrooke Street a corridor of art—"Corridart" was what Charney named it—and, according to the official Olympic book published by COJO, "a red carpet to the Olympic Park." The harmony of body and mind was to be symbolized by the display of sport and art tied together in and by one of Montreal's best-known streets.

The events leading to the construction of Olympic Park began, publically, at a press conference held by Mayor Jean Drapeau in August 1972. Obviously a great deal had transpired, privately, before the press conference. Present was the French architect, Roger Taillibert, whom Mayor Drapeau had already selected as the architect of the Olympics. Why Taillibert? Drapeau had been impressed, on a visit to Paris, with Taillibert's Parc des Prince Stadium. "I noticed," said Drapeau, "that it was something out of the ordinary, something that was later confirmed by expert engineers, who said it was something out of the ordinary."

Along with their first glimpse of the Olympic architect, the public got their first glimpse of the Olympics; Taillibert presented, in rough outline, his design. *(Figure 70)*

Unfortunately, Taillibert's Olympic buildings, along with the Olympic Village, the vast complex to house the athletes designed by Roger D'Astous and Luc Durand, would eventually present not only the 1976 Olympics, but also the City of Montreal, in a very unfavourable light. A special relationship had developed between the mayor and his chosen architect: all of Taillibert's ideas would be treated as precious artistic conceptions, their artistic integrity carefully pro-

Figure 70. 1976 Olympic Games, Montreal. Model of the Olympic Stadium and the Velodrome. Roger Taillibert, Architect.

Figure 71. Aerial view of the Olympic Stadium and the Velodrome. The Stadium tower was not completed for the games. Roger Taillibert, Architect.

Figure 72. Interior of the Velodrome.

tected from outside interference by Mayor Drapeau himself. Costs escalated as the Quebec construction industry, when not on strike, tried to put up the huge Olympic stadium and velodrome—buildings characterized by large curving concrete planes and asymmetrical forms. The construction system was one of great complexity; each pre-cast concrete segment was, in some sense, unique and in need of special attention. The demands made of the men and materials were, at the very least, Olympian.

The velodrome, which was to house the track for Olympic cycling, came to look like "some giant Paleozoic trilobite come to rest at the bottom of the sea," in the words of architect John Hix. A concrete shell spanned 177 metres (approximately 580 feet), branching out from a single fixed support at one end to three supports on the other. The roof contained five rows of long, gently-arched skylights, making the building look from above like a prehistoric animal. From inside, the light and space are undeniably dramatic, something which is "often the case with structures which struggle with almost impossibly difficult tasks" in the words of engineer Paul Sandori who analysed the building. *(Figures 71, 72)*

No less dramatic was the Olympic stadium, seating capacity 69,000. Thirty-four concrete ribs, placed along an oval perimeter of 480 metres (1580 feet) on its long axis, formed the structure of the walls and roof of the stadium. These ribs were designed to cantilever out between 62 and 82 metres (205-269 feet) over the centre of the stadium, to define and support an oval-shaped ring which would house lighting and mechanical equipment. This oval ring would be tilted upwards towards a concrete tower which would in turn lean over the stadium to "support" a removable plastic roof for the stadium which would fit along the perimeter of the inclined oval opening. The dimensions of the tower were in keeping with the theme established elsewhere: it was to be over 170 metres (560 feet) high, and lean 53 metres (175 feet) over the stadium. *(Figures 73, 74)*

Figure 73. The Olympic Stadium under construction.

Figure 74. The Olympic Stadium during the 1976 Games.

Figure 75. The Olympic Village, built to house the athletes. Roger D'Astous and Luc Durand, Architects.

The Olympic Village to house the athletes was located across Sherbrooke Street on the south side. It bore a *striking* resemblance to the Baie des Anges residential complex on the Cote D'Azur in France, the Montreal buildings offering the same pyramidal shape and corridors on the outside which had worked so well in the south of France. *(Figure 75)*

At the time Melvin Charney was offered the contract for Corridart, "We were beginning," he says, "to suspect the *quantities* of money that were being squandered into this grandiose scheme." Indeed, even in retrospect it is difficult to comprehend the amount of money that it cost to build only *parts* of the Olympic buildings which Taillibert had originally presented in August 1972. In making his case and that of Montreal to the International Olympic Committee in 1970, Drapeau had stressed that Montreal would put on a "modest" games on a human scale, at a cost of $124 million, maximum. At the August 1972 press conference, Taillibert, in an aside to a journalist, had estimated that the Olympic stadium would cost around $60 million.

By the time the stadium was complete (but without the tower), $60 million was only enough to build two parking garages on the stadium site, although that price did include a fountain which Taillibert insisted on, at a reported cost of $8 million. Money? "Money is all Canadians and North Americans think about," said Taillibert, "money, money, money. It doesn't interest me at all. When you look at the Eiffel Tower, what remains to think about? The honorarium Eiffel received or the structure he created?"

As the costs rose for the stadium, Mayor Drapeau refused to allow the artist's conception to be changed in any way. There was shock and outrage when the final cost of the stadium was announced: $650 million. In the oft-quoted example, Seattle, Washington built a 60,000-seat domed stadium at the time of the Montreal Olympics for $60 million, the cost of those two parking garages. Alter the design? "The design is a work of art," explained Mayor Drapeau. "Never, never, never did we think of changing the design."

From an original contract of $12.3 million for the construction of the velodrome, costs escalated to $70 million. The scandal-tinged Olympic Village escalated from $30 million to $80 million before the city expropriated the buildings from the original developer /owner. From an original cost estimate of $124 million, the Olympics had escalated to an estimated $1.4 billion. And the stadium still had no roof; construction on the tower had only begun.

"The story," says Melvin Charney, recalling his involvement with the Olympics, "is unbelievable." Out of a total Olympic budget which he estimates as closer to $2 billion, he received a budget of $400,000, four months before the Olympic games were to begin, to create Corridart. "The budget was low," he says, "so I felt that, in order to stretch it the five and a half miles, I absolutely had to use the street as an exhibition of itself. Sherbrooke Street is *full* of interesting things; the idea was to highlight these things."

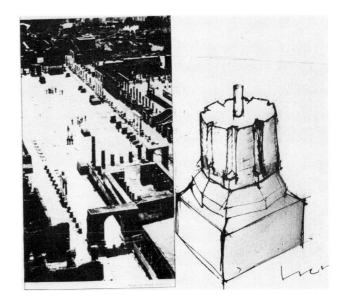

Figure 76. Corridart, Montreal. To anchor the scaffolding, counterweights were designed in the form of doric column bases suggesting the ruins of a "politique de grandeur." Melvin Charney, Architect.

Eleven days before the Olympics were to begin, Corridart officially opened. Conceptually, there were three "zones," although to the west and east of the central zone, Charney hoped that Sherbooke Street itself would provide the attractions, as his budget did not really enable him to enliven the street along its full length.

Thus, from Atwater to Park Avenue, to the west of the central zone, Sherbrooke Street traversed the city centre: new and old hotels; offices and clubs; the Montreal Museum of Fine Arts and Montreal's best-known art galleries. From La Fontaine Park to the Olympic Park, to the east of the central zone, was what Charney calls "the mindless strip development &whiché was allowed to take over this part of the city since the '40s — the drive-ins and instant flash that articulate a show of their own."

The central and principal zone of Corridart, the two kilometre-long part of the street between Park Avenue and La Fontaine Park, was an area of Montreal which still retained, in Charney's words, "the original sense of the place." Here are to be found the Ecole des Beaux-Arts and the Ecole d'Architecture, while the side streets were filled, in the words of the architect, "with a history of artist studios, cafés and cinemas where ideas were thrashed out and art was produced." Correspondingly, Corridart was to be most dense in this zone.

Of over four hundred entries submitted in an open competition, sixteen were selected and placed in this area. Banners hung between lamp posts created a street festival atmosphere of poetry readings, clowns and jugglers, and an outdoor café where theatre was performed.

Legende des Artistes, by Françoise Sullivan, David Moore, and Jean-Serge Champagne, was a "salute to the houses where legends are born," a series of twelve wooden boxes mounted at eye level with carefully detailed photo-montages of the artists and their environment, the immediate area of the central zone of Corridart. Using the three-dimensional volume of the boxes and a rich layering of images, the artists were able to create a series of metaphors for the richness of imagery and emotion which characterizes an urban neighbourhood.

Teletron, by Michael Haslam, consisted of a pair of old telephone booths with a neon sign flashing "teletron" overhead. Picking up one of the telephones, one could hear the tape-recorded voices both of the artists themselves and of people interviewed on the street talking about the artwork and issues of contemporary importance.

To support what he chose to call "documents," Charney rented metal scaffolding and secured it into special concrete counterweights which he had designed to look like the bases of ruined Doric columns. The "documents" (the term suggested a legal case) were mounted on the scaffolding, and came in two forms.

The first was that of photographs of people and events in the history of Sherbrooke Street. There were pictures of residents past and present along with details of their lives; "monuments," such as Mckim Mead and White's Mount Royal Club (1904-7); and important processions of the past along the street, such as the one on St. Jean Baptiste Day. There were pictures of events of every kind, from important celebrations to gruesome car accidents. *(Figure 76)*

The second sort of document consisted of a series of giant pointing hands cast out of bright red plastic. The hands were mounted on the scaffolding in such a way that they could be pivoted and pointed at the architect's discretion. Ostensibly to "guide" people through the museum, the pointing hands actually went much further. One pointed towards a typically hand-crafted, nineteenth-century wooden balcony detail, alerting the public to positive urban design features which were fast disappearing. Others, such as the one pointing to the highrise apartment building which had replaced the historic Van Horne Mansion and the one pointing at the Montreal Museum of Fine Arts, angered owners and trustees of these buildings to the point of letters and phone calls calling for the offending objects to be moved. Charney invariably complied simply by turning the hands on their pivots to point in another direction. *(Figures 77, 78)*

Charney's strongest gesture occurred on a corner lot in the central zone, a lot which had been cleared of housing for an institutional project still unbuilt by the time of the Olympics. Using the same rented scaffolding as a frame, the architect built a rough plywood, full-size facade which was the mirror image of the houses on the opposite corner. Although open to interpretation on a number of levels, this gesture was the centrepiece of Charney's exposé of municipal indifference and even destruction in Montreal. *(Figures 79, 80, 81)*

The entire Corridart exhibit had been in place for only a week, from July 6th to 13th, when Montreal's municipal workers were ordered by Drapeau's office to destroy it in the middle of the night. Why? The exhibition was a "regrettable failure," in the words of Mayor Drapeau, "an incredible pollution of Sherbrooke Street." Driving along Sherbrooke Street the Sunday before Corridart was destroyed, the Mayor described his reaction as "shocked," "humiliated" and "insulted." When the Olympics opened on July 17th, there was no trace of Corridart.

In almost every respect, the Olympic Park/Village and Corridart represented antithetical notions about architecture. Seeing architecture on the scale of the Olympics as an exclusive venue for personal impulse, Taillibert really had very little interest in Montreal, or the rest of the country for that matter. "Tomorrow's architecture," explained Taillibert, "will be acquatic."

Corridart, on the other hand, evidenced what Charney likes to call the "necessity of architecture," architecture as a kind of cultural fabric, at once the foreground of and background to community life. Accepting no limitations except those which he imposed on himself, Taillibert's designs demanded an amount of money well beyond local means.

With a minimum of money and technology, Corridart celebrated the possibility (or, again, "necessity") of public life. It pointed directly to the current dilemma

Figures 77,78. (opposite page) Corridart scaffolding on Sherbrooke Street: historical photographs and "the street as an exhibition of itself."

Figure 79. A corner of Sherbrooke Street as found: on the left, 19th century housing stock; on the right, an empty lot left by demolition.

Figure 80. The street as imagined: a photographic reconstruction.

Figure 81. Sherbrooke Street rebuilt: Charney's strongest gesture, ripped down along with the rest of Corridart on orders from the mayor. Melvin Charney, Architect.

of North American cities where, "the public content of the street," as Charney puts it, "is being removed systematically." Particularly because of the way that the municipal government responded to it, Corridart and its "documents" will be remembered both as a celebration of public life in Montreal, and as a criticism of the turn that public life in that city had taken by 1976.

IV   Design, Guidelines, and the Changing Forms of Public Life

Not all the changes to public space that have occurred in Canada over the past decade have been a function of the kind of neglect and destruction implicitly criticized by Melvin Charney in his Corridart project. Nor have they been strictly the kind of reverential, piece-by-piece restoration undertaken in Ottawa's Sussex Drive courts, or the kind of wholesale salvage and recycling operations underway at Vancouver's Granville Island. Despite the publicity surrounding such projects, most recent architecture in Canadian cities has consisted of new construction. Indeed, much of this construction has been on a scale unprecedented in this country, involving immense public transportation systems and enormous tracts of privately-owned and highly-valued downtown land. In many cases, large segments of the urban fabric have been redeveloped, with only a few features or buildings selected for retention.

What has happened, however, is that the high profile of rehabilitation and infill projects has, together with the increasing scale and complexity of urban life, promoted an awareness and an appreciation of public spaces that respond to cultural practices and aspirations. While the awareness of new forms of public life has derived in part from an architectural vogue, it has in some instances resulted from city and provincial government guidelines that have been established to protect and enhance the historical, social, and urbane qualities of Canadian cities.

Ironically, the scale of much of the new development has been in large measure a result of government policies, particularly at the federal level. The post-war policies of the Central Mortgage and Housing Corporation fostered the growth of colossal international private development corporations, making Canadian-based companies like Olympia & York and Cadillac Fairview among the largest developers in North America. The massive redevelopment of which these developers are capable has called forth the complex zoning by-laws and planning guidelines that occupy increasingly the agendas of municipal councils.

The result of renewed interest in history and context, combined with such guidelines, is that developers and architects have begun mixing less lucrative uses with highly profitable ones, less efficient but historically venerable buildings with new super-efficient structures, and public areas with commercially profitable leasable space. Such projects as Calgary's Plus 15 pedestrian system, Toronto's Spadina Subway, Vancouver's Robson Square, Toronto's Eaton Centre, and Montreal's Complexe Desjardins, while expressive of technological and economic optimism, reflect different aspects of a growing awareness of the larger urban and cultural order.

Plus 15, Calgary

In urban systems like Calgary's downtown pedestrian plan and Toronto's Spadina subway line, the scale and complexity of the projects has required a generation of planning and implementation, and the involvement of scores of different interest groups, professionals, artists, and ultimately on a daily basis, millions of citizens.

Calgary has encouraged high-rise, high-density redevelopment in the downtown core. However in 1970, the city implemented a policy intended to mitigate the effects of such redevelopment. Hailed as the most comprehensive system of its kind in North America, Plus 15's main feature is a network of bridges, plazas, and climate-controlled walkways to and through buildings. The passages are raised one level (or 15 feet, hence the name, Plus 15) above ground to allow for the uninterrupted passage of traffic below. (Actually the height has been raised three feet higher, due to traffic accidents involving 15-foot high bridges and crane-carrying trucks.) *(Figure 82)*

The Plus 15 system is only possible in a city like Calgary. The amount of new high-rise construction ensures that connections can be readily accommodated in new designs, and that the developers of buildings across from one another can split the costs of providing bridges. Unlike Montreal and Toronto, cities which have routed pedestrians into climate-controlled tunnels under neighbouring towers, Calgary's high water table precluded an underground system.

The bridges have been installed in buildings within a section of downtown called the "must area." Developers of new buildings in the "must area" *must* link into the system at their own expense, or pay the city to have it done for them. Conversely, buildings outside the "must area" can earn extra floor space allowances if they provide Plus 15 bridges to adjacent buildings. The formula for the bonus has been: extra floor space = 30

Figure 82. Interior of Plus 15 bridge between Provincial Court and Remand Centre, Calgary. Jack Long and the New Street Group, Architects.

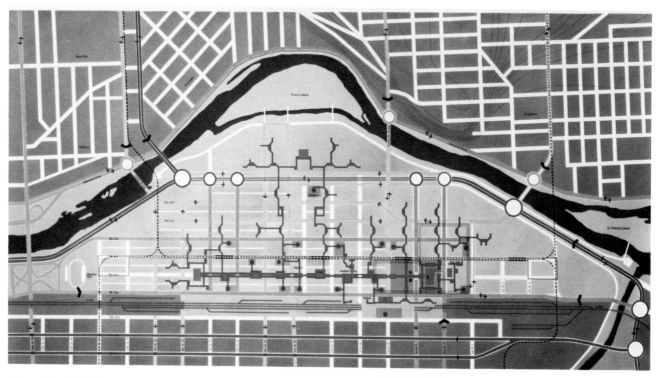

Figure 83. 1967 Plan of Pedestrian System, including mall, lanes and Plus 15 system, Calgary. Affleck, Desbarats, Dimakopoulos and Sise, Architects.

times the area of the bridge. Still undergoing redefinition, the system is now being modified to better coordinate with other systems for car and pedestrian movement, and to achieve other downtown planning aims.

Why design a separate system for pedestrians? Apart from the obvious discomfort of harsh winter weather, the City of Calgary Planning Department's 1969 "Downtown Development Guidelines" justified Plus 15 by claiming that it would "ensure adequate provision for the pedestrian . . . without infringing unduly upon the rights of the individual to obtain a fair development of his property." Thus, just as the extent to which a developer could cover and occupy his land is regulated, so too is the nature of public access to the Plus 15 realm. An "Activity Policy" determined that half the space fronting on the walkways had to be for "retail, cultural, entertainment, or amusement" uses. For an apartment building, the policy required that only a quarter of the frontage be for "activity."

The pedestrian system is not limited to the street-crossing bridges. The original plan drawn up by Affleck, Desbarats, Dimakopoulos, Lebensold and Sise in 1967 emphasized the development of former lane spaces between the backs and sides of buildings for pedestrian use as well. The second floors of buildings would be required, both by the "Activity Policy" and by the pervasiveness of the pedestrian zone, to provide a new type of semi-public space linking the bridges to other bridges and to plazas located in the middle of blocks. *(Figure 83)*

Although the Plus 15 system was conceived of as a policy of benefit primarily to pedestrians, it is essentially controlled by, and of considerable benefit to, the private sector. For one of the drawbacks of establishing a system so completely predicated on new construction is that the interests of small property owners are not addressed. Their inability to link into the system has had a detrimental effect on street-level shops and on Calgary's street life generally.

Nevertheless, Harold Hanen, a Senior Planner in Calgary's Planning Department at the time when Plus 15 was first conceived, continues to endorse the city's pedestrian policy, insisting that, "Plus 15 has had a very positive effect on architecture in Calgary. It has established the interdependence of buildings on each other, and tends to make architects less arrogant, more aware of each other's buildings."

The strengths and weaknesses of the system are amply demonstrated by the Toronto-Dominion Square's Devonian Gardens, to date the only major interior space specifically designed to fit into the Plus 15 network. The bank's black steel and glass tower sits

Figure 84. Toronto-Dominion Square, Calgary. Fronting on the 8th Avenue pedestrian mall, but above it and behind the dark, sloping glass, the Devonian Gardens. J. H. Cook Architects and Engineers, in association with Skidmore Owings and Merrill, Architects.

Figure 85. Interior of the Devonian Gardens, Toronto Dominion Square, Calgary.

Figure 86. The Hudson's Bay Store, street-level arcade, 8th Avenue Mall, Calgary.

atop a four-storey podium on 3rd Street S.W., between 7th Avenue and 8th Avenue. Eighth Avenue is itself a pedestrian precinct created by partial closure to automobile traffic. *(Figure 84)*

From the Plus 15 level upward, much of this podium has been devoted to an indoor garden open to the public. Landscaped terraces rise through several levels, and walkways criss-cross the mass of vegetation which has grown into a dense jungle. Warm sunshine streams through the sloped glass during even the most severe winter weather. The gardens are used by lunching office workers, and include a small playground and a space for displaying art. *(Figure 85)*

In marked contrast to the nearby Hudson's Bay store with its gracious, street-level arcades, the T-D Square satisfies the city's rules for pedestrian movement, but only insofar as the rules contribute revenue to its retail activities. The Devonian Gardens, its one real amenity, is accessible exclusively via a shopping mall, and is all but invisible from 8th Avenue below because of the Square's relentlessly dark glass surface. *(Figure 86)*

The ability of Plus 15 to accommodate itself to a non-commercial setting is illustrated by the connections it provides between a number of government buildings located east of the commercial part of Calgary's downtown core. Here the Provincial Court and Remand Centre, designed by Jack Long and the New Street Group (1975), is connected by Plus 15 bridges to two other institutions of fairly recent construction, the Police Station and the Public Library. These latter are connected to City Hall, a pre-World War I sandstone structure, via its Administration Building Annex.

It is one thing for stores to be off the same hallway as the Devonian Gardens, but is clearly another for a remand centre/court house and police station to be sharing hallways with a public library. It is especially incongruous to walk out from the lobby of the library into the halls of a police station and to see uniformed police on their way to court. Even more disconcerting are the hallways themselves, a concatenation of concrete, bullet-proof glass, steel, aluminum, planters, and displays, separating the mid-block Plus 15 zone from the back lane where prisoners are delivered in police cars for detention and trial. *(Figure 87)*

The Court and Remand Centre's architectural adjustment to the Plus 15 is necessarily more abrupt than that of commercial buildings, like the Toronto-Dominion Square. The low-rise Court and Remand Centre building is organized visually as if the ground level were a basement and the second level were the ground level. Downstairs is the entrance to the jail; the jail's administrative offices present a blank concrete wall to cars speeding by on the one-way street. The second level contains a large lobby encircled by courtrooms. Inserted between the entry to the Remand Centre and its upper floors of dormitories and cells, the Court House generously accommodates the Plus 15 that is routed through it by providing a comfortably large atrium, with refreshingly low lighting levels and casual furniture. It is a space that seems to address the pedestrian, pausing on his walk, say, from City Hall to the Board of Education building across the street as much as it replies to the functional need for lobby space for the courts. *(Figures 88, 89)*

Figure 87. View of the Provincial Court and Remand Centre from across the street, Calgary. Jack Long and the New Street Group, Architects.

Figure 88. Provincial Court and Remand Centre, interior view of the Courthouse atrium, Calgary. The atrium is connected with the Plus 15 system.

Figure 89. Front of Provincial Court and Remand Centre, viewed from Plus 15 across the street, Calgary.

While Calgary's Plus 15 may represent an improvement on Toronto and Montreal's subterranean concourses and Edmonton's ''Pedway'' (a little-implemented system which is randomly above, below, and at ground level), it suffers from a lack of ingenuity. Traditionally, a separation between pedestrians and vehicular traffic has been motivated by the double aims of increasing the efficiency of the roadway, and creating an idyllic promenade, far removed from the exhaust fumes. Although it is generally agreed that vehicular efficiency is best served by a grid pattern of streets, there is no reason for pedestrians to be similarly regimented. Despite providing a respite from car traffic, the Plus 15 system is as rigidly gridded as the abandoned sidewalks below, and has not fulfilled its original promise of providing pedestrian oases in the middle of blocks.

Figure 90. A drawing from New York's visionary twenties: ''General view of a city square showing the additional possibility of a second level of pedestrian traffic at the height of a ten-storey setback.'' Harvey Wiley Corbett, Architect.

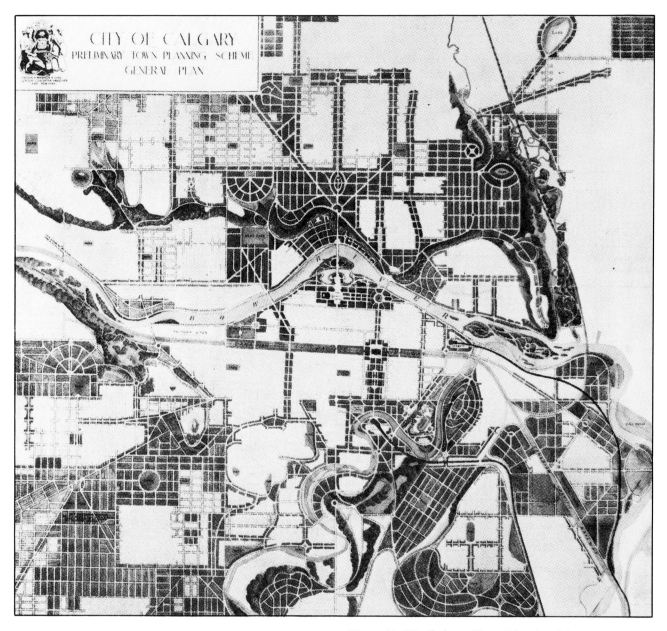

Figure 91. "Preliminary Town Planning Scheme — General Plan," 1914, Calgary. Thomas Mawson, town planner.

Town planner Thomas Mawson, whose 1914 plan for Calgary envisioned an ideal garden-city, would recognize few of his dreams for winding, treed promenades in the Plus 15 bridges. The Plus 15 realm is too often an impoverished version of a well-regulated public sidewalk system, and the bridges have too often fostered an unwarranted degree of control of collective space by private interests. *(Figures 90, 91)*

Spadina Subway, Toronto

Toronto, too, had planned for the common good in anticipation of future growth. As early as 1909, a subway system was proposed. The Bloor Street Viaduct was designed to carry subway trains, as well as cars and horse-drawn carriages, across the Don Valley. The Yonge Street Subway line, Canada's first, opened in 1954.

Not long after the Yonge line was in operation, the city's Metropolitan Planning Board, in anticipation of even greater growth, proposed that the Spadina Subway line be built in conjunction with a new expressway. The idea at the time was first to install the largely above-ground line as a sort of commuter rail line, and later to build the north and southbound expressway lanes on either side. However, over twenty years were to pass before the opening of the Spadina line's eight stations in 1978. The delay was due in part to virulent citizen opposition to the expressway, and to the destruction of neighbourhoods and homes.

In 1963 work began on the northern terminus of the expressway at Highway 401. By 1966, the Spadina Expressway, was finished from Wilson to Lawrence. Approximately half of the eight hundred houses slated for demolition had been torn down.

As the expressway approached the older, more densely settled areas to the south, citizen protest reached a crescendo. Many shared Marshall McLuhan's view that the high-speed route, slicing through established neighbourhoods, would be "a cement kimono for Toronto." The subway was to be the silk lining, but few were won over by its appeal.

Public hearings began in 1970 with the result that the Provincial Government stepped in to stop the expressway. "If we are building a transportation system to serve the automobile," Premier William Davis declared to the legislature in 1971, "the Spadina Expressway would be a good place to start. But if we are building a transportation system to serve people, the Spadina Expressway is a good place to stop." For the next four years, attention shifted from the completed-but-unopened portion of the expressway between Wilson and Lawrence avenues to the excavated-but-unbuilt portion south from Lawrence to Eglinton Avenue, the infamous "Spadina ditch." In the context of the 1971 campaign, which Premier Davis won in part because of his promise to stop the expressway, U.S. architect Buckminster Fuller proposed a linear village of housing and stores to be built in the ditch. "Project Spadina," as the Fuller scheme was called, was designed to fill the sides of the ditch with terraced, low-rise

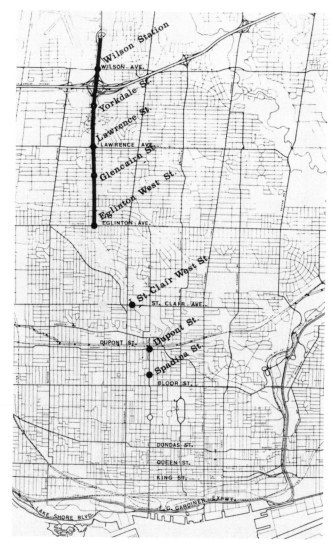

Figure 92. Map of Toronto showing stations on the Spadina subway line, Spadina Expressway indicated by heavy line. Toronto Transit Commission Staff, under the direction and approval of the Commissioners.

buildings, thereby inverting what Fuller characterized as "the glass cliffs of the usual high-rises."

Like many campaign promises, Project Spadina was quickly forgotten, leaving Metro Council, the municipal body governing Toronto and its suburbs, to take charge. Metro Council, which has traditionally favoured suburban interests, wanted to pave the ditch, open it as an "arterial road," and run the Spadina Subway right down its median strip. By then, however, the Spadina alignment, although precisely the one recommended in 1956, was only one of twenty alternative subway routes being considered. After further study, Metro's Executive Committee voted to change the subway alignment to Bathurst Street where the city's ravines would be less disturbed, fewer houses would be destroyed, and the subway would run through areas of greater population density. *(Figure 92)*

In considering alternative routes, the City was confronted with the issue which had plagued the subway/ expressway from the start: an expressway is ideally situated on the suburban fringe, while a subway works best in the heart of the urban fabric. Despite this central point, Metro Council chose in 1972, as a final "compromise," to construct the Spadina Subway down the abandoned ditch.

Subway construction had been advancing along the centre of the ditch for five months when, in January 1975, the Davis government agreed to pave it. The paving was made palatable by the condition that from Lawrence to Eglinton avenues, the Spadina Expressway would be called an "arterial road with limited access." Since arterial roads, like Yonge Street, are merely wide city streets that do not have limited access, the semantic sleight-of-hand was widely recognized for the contradiction it was.

Nonetheless, on September 7, 1976, travelling along the freshly-paved road for the first time, drivers found that south of Lawrence, the William R. Allen Expressway was duly marked as the "William R. Allen Arterial Road." And because this road dead ends abruptly at a traffic light on Eglinton Avenue West, drivers waiting in the long rush-hour line-ups had ample time to contemplate the Spadina line's new, air-conditioned trains travelling up and down the median strip.

In response to criticism of the sterility of Toronto's earlier engineer-designed stations, the Toronto Transit Commission (T.T.C.) decided to involve not only architects but local artists in the design of the Spadina stations. Kendal and Glencairn were allotted to Adamson Associates, Dupont and Lawrence to Dunlop Farrow Aitken (DFA), and Eglinton and Yorkdale to Arthur Erickson Associates. The T.T.C. meanwhile reserved the right to design what it considered the two most "difficult" stations, their difficulty being deemed a function of technical rather than architectural or urban design parameters. An independent art consultant, Nina Wright, was retained to conduct a feasibility study on the choice of art for the stations.

By the time the stations were to be designed, demolition of historic buildings had become sufficiently unpopular that Adamson Associates devoted considerable effort to preserving the turn-of-the-century Romanesque Revival house that stood on the site of the

Figure 93. Construction of Spadina Subway Station, at Kendal Avenue, Toronto. Moving the house on steel rails. Adamson Associates, Architects.

southern-most station. The house was placed on steel beams and rolled aside while the underground station was constructed. Afterwards, like an elaborate stage set, the partially-gutted house was rolled back into place and refurbished to serve as the flagship Spadina Station. The former front lawn was replaced by a brick patio, and the house now sits several inches below its original level. Although these changes were the source of some criticism from architectural historians who felt that the house's relationship to the ground should have been more accurately maintained, the resulting streetscape looked much as it had previously, putting to rest fears that the new subway line would disrupt the character of Spadina Road. Appropriately, the art installed at the Spadina Station is a Joyce Wieland quilt, "Barren Ground Caribou," a work of similarly gentle preservationist leanings. *(Figures 93, 94)*

Stations at Dupont and at Lawrence (both by Dunlop Farrow Aitken) make their presence felt at street level, but as at Spadina, they do so in ways appropriate to their context. At Dupont, the presence of the underground subway stop is emphatically announced above ground by its entrances: two arresting, transparent pavilions framed with bright orange metal straps and placed on diagonally opposite corners. In an area where housing, shops, and light industry are mixed with few common architectural qualities, the two identically-formed pavilions help to define the intersection. *(Figure 95)*

At Lawrence, as at the other stations along the median strip, the design challenge was to create a sense of place within a landscape in perpetual motion. The use of the Spadina median, with its long history of conflict, as a site for public architecture, seemed to demand

Figure 94. Completed Spadina Station, with house back in place. Adamson Associates, Architects.

Figure 95. Exterior of Dupont Subway Station, Spadina Line, Toronto. Dunlop Farrow Aitken, Architects.

Figure 96. Exterior of Lawrence Subway Station showing bus platforms, Spadina Line, Toronto. Dunlop Farrow Aitken, Architects.

Figure 97. Interior of Lawrence Station, subway platform.

extraordinary gestures. DFA again used bright orange pavilions on either side of the street with spectacular effect. In this case, however, the pavilions are not identical. From the larger one, on the south side of Lawrence, "Spacing . . . Aerial Highways," a vibrantly-coloured tile mural by Claude Breeze, extends out and over the Allen Expressway as it passes under Lawrence Avenue. Like the mural, the placement of the station's bus platforms out over the expressway takes advantage of the dramatic potential offered by the intersection of different modes of transportation. *(Figures 96, 97, 98)*

Figure 98. Exterior of Lawrence Station, showing Claude Breeze mural.

Figure 99. Yorkdale Station, Toronto, Exterior. Arthur Erickson Associates, Architects.

The most extraordinary of all the stations along the median is the Yorkdale Station, designed by Arthur Erickson Associates. Yorkdale is the slickest transit station of any kind in Canada, with a unique location adjacent to a shopping plaza. Architecturally, it relates only to the median strip and to the subway trains that drive along it, not to the shopping centre and commuter parking lots it serves. *(Figure 99)*

Shoppers arriving by transit have to cross a vast, windy, shopping centre parking lot to get from the station to the mall, a situation which might have been mitigated had Hans Blumenfeld, a planner involved with the Spadina line, prevailed over the plaza owners' attitude towards public transportation:

> I got the T.T.C. and Yorkdale people (Trizec Equities) together, and I tried to get the shopping centre people to put a direct entrance (from the subway station) into their

shopping centre. But they were adamant. They said, "No, we already have all our leases, and our experience is that only 7% of our people come by public transit.

In other negotiations with the City regarding parking space for commuters from neighbouring areas, Trizec offered space — over half a kilometre from the station. As if anticipating the plaza's indifference to it, the Yorkdale Station is, except for an unavoidable pedestrian bridge extended out over the expressway to the plaza's parking lot, coolly detached from the plaza. *(Figure 100)*

Modelled after the subway trains, the silvery stainless steel-covered platform glamorizes the industrial image of the subway, making it seem as urbane and sophisticated to ride the T.T.C. as to shop in the elegant steel and glass boutiques downtown on Bloor Street. Trains emerging from the Yorkdale stop, with its curved steel cladding and subway car-like windows, appear to glide as naturally as snakes gliding out of a former skin.

Figures 101,102. Yorkdale Station, Toronto. Interior.

Figure 100. Yorkdale Station, Toronto. Aerial view showing bridge to Yorkdale shopping plaza in foreground, right.

From the perspective of motorists driving by, the icy and sleek Yorkdale Station monumentalizes the passage of trains through it.

Yorkdale Station's platform is, like the Lawrence Station mural, an instance where the architects' and the artists' work are closely synchronized. Delicate steel ribs support a vaulted glass roof which wraps down over the north and south ends of the platform, allowing views out over the train tracks beyond. The steel ribs hold a neon sculpture by Michael Hayden composed of hoops of colours of the spectrum, which are illuminated sequentially, triggered by the arrival of trains. The illumination is best appreciated when the sky is dark. Hayden's "Arc en Ciel," a mechanical rainbow of lights "travelling" against the glass of the ceiling, serves as an analogue to the movement of trains through the space and alludes to the sky overhead. *(Figures 101, 102, 103)*

Figure 103. Yorkdale Station, Toronto, Roof showing Michael Hayden's neon sculpture, "Arc en Ciel." Arthur Erickson Associates, Architects.

In its idealized expression of subway travel, the Yorkdale Station clearly raises problems that remain unresolved about the Spadina system as a whole. The station's ability to stand on its own architecturally, dependent only on the trains' operation, is a reminder of the line's isolation from the established settlement that is ordinarily its lifeblood. In contrast to the subway systems of Vienna and Paris, where engineers, artists, and architects have collaborated to design systems that serve as models of urban design, the Spadina line bears witness to the consequences of politicians, planners, developers and architects independently pursuing their respective concerns.

Robson Square and Provincial Law Courts, Vancouver

Vancouver's Robson Square and Provincial Law Courts, Toronto's Eaton Centre and Commerce Court, and Montreal's Complexe Desjardins demonstrate both positive and negative aspects of urban renewal. These recent large-scale developments have provided the central areas of these cities with new types of semi-public and public space. In accommodating the interests of large and complex clients, the designers of these mega-developments have attempted, with varying degrees of success, to balance economies of scale with vibrant images of social life.

Robson Square and the Provincial Law Courts (Arthur Erickson Associates, 1980) form a new government and civic centre for Vancouver, occupying three blocks of prime downtown real estate owned by the B.C. government. Running from north to south, Blocks 51/61/71, as they were referred to prior to the new construction, became notorious for the debate that raged over whether the land should be used for a 55-storey tower, or a public park or square. *(Figure 104)*

The new Law Courts have also replaced courts previously housed in the Neo-classical building at the northern end of Block 51 with an all-new complex on Block 71. The former Court House is being restored and has been designated for use by the Vancouver Art Gallery. Named in honour of a nineteenth-century premier of British Columbia, John Robson, the development is long and narrow and bracketed on both ends by law court buildings, the one a fine example of nineteenth-century architect Francis Rattenbury's work, the other representative of the recent architecture of Arthur Erickson Associates. Together, the two buildings invite comparison of architectural styles and social attitudes as they have evolved over the past century. *(Figure 105)*

The portion of Block 51 south of the Rattenbury Court House has been carved out to create Robson Square. Lined on its east and west edges by restaurants and food concessions, the Square extends southward under Robson Street to the mid-point of Block 61. From there, a low-rise B.C. government office building extends still further southward, spanning Smithe Street, and ending just as it reaches Block 71. Block 71 is blanketed by the new Law Courts building, an eight-storey edifice characterized by its stepped concrete frame structure. Arthur Erickson's predilection for creating buildings as landscape, seen earlier in his proposal for the National Gallery competition, has found its largest-scale realization to date in Robson Square. In

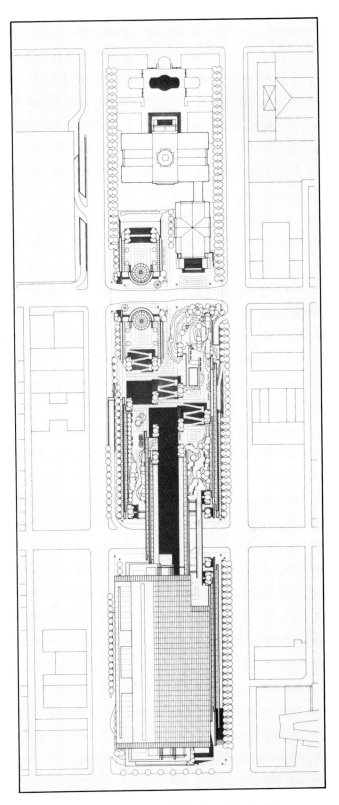

Figure 104. Robson Square and the Law Courts, Vancouver, Site plan, Blocks 51/61/71. Arthur Erickson Associates, Architects.

Figure 105. Robson Square and the Law Courts, Vancouver,
Aerial view. Arthur Erickson Associates, Architects.

Figure 106. Robson Square, Vancouver, View looking north.

a few more years, the concrete walls of the government office building will have all but disappeared behind the vast plantings along its terraces. *(Figure 106)*

The size and southward bias of Robson Square's park and paths provide a dramatic forecourt to the Law Courts. A sophisticated series of visual and sensual cues draws the visitor through the complex. "Stramps," a hybrid stair/ramp suggestive of the ceremonial architecture of ancient civilizations, make what are, in actuality, extreme level changes seem enticing. Thousands of plants and two spectacularly-engineered waterfalls address the approaching pedestrian, compelling him

Figure 107. Government Office Complex, Smithe Street overpass, and the Law Courts, Vancouver. Arthur Erickson Associates, Architects.

along for three blocks through a man-made landscape with much of the interest and complexity of the natural environment. *(Figure 107)*

The natural-seeming flow of space ends abruptly at Nelson Street. A short stair descends to an ordinary city sidewalk where the concrete end-wall of a very ordinary building is all that one can see. Despite the tantalizing suggestion that this masterfully-contoured landscape is a continuous or, even better, a typical piece of downtown Vancouver, it is in fact all too finite and unique, terminated on both ends by buildings which are raised significantly above street level. *(Figure 108)*

Like all modern inventions, the project challenges preconceptions of the ways things have been or ought to be. The two end buildings now face each other across Robson Square, rather than the streets on which they sit. The definition of city blocks and streets has been overruled by pedestrian passages that have been made above and below ground level.

The glass-roof lobby of the Law Courts where, by Arthur Erickson's own description, "Justice must not only be done but be seen to be done," is a huge, theatrical space. The flat public passageway is in notable contrast to the terraces of court rooms, and the concealed corridors beyond which judges and the accused travel, segregated for security purposes. There is nothing for the casual visitor to do in the lobby but to marvel at the scale of the space. Similarly, the public space of Robson Square, severed from casual sidewalk access by its complex arrangement of levels, suggests ancient Roman fora or Greek amphitheatres, and appears to be intended for occasions of extreme formality. *(Figure 109)*

Figure 108. Law Courts, Vancouver, corner of Nelson and Howe Streets.

Figure 109. Law Courts, Vancouver, Interior, Public Lobby. Arthur Erickson Associates, Architects.

Robson Square offers an image of the City as a place of serene but austere beauty. No discordant elements, no jarring electric signs, no traffic, no mullions to interrupt the glassy expanse of the Law Courts' roof. It holds up an ascetic standard to what Arthur Erickson has called "our trash-oriented society." He comments that, "Our surroundings, most of our food, what we read, what we see in films, hear in music, desensitizes our perceptions. We learn an indifference to things rather than a respect and love of our surroundings."

By imposing this ascetic standard on the surrounding area rather than accepting cues from it, the architecture attempts to dictate exactly what our perceptions of it should be.

Eaton Centre, Toronto

Toronto's Eaton Centre (Bregman & Hamann and Zeidler Partnership, 1981) also engulfs its site, and in so doing, sets the tone for the surrounding area. Like most North American shopping malls, Eaton Centre does not itself have a centre. It consists of a new Eaton store which anchors the development on its northern end, two high-rise office towers, and the 274-metre-long (900 foot) glass-roofed Galleria. Flanked on both sides by three levels of stores, the Galleria links the flagship Eaton store to the century-old Simpson's store which, although not part of the development, effectively serves as the project's southern boundary. *(Figure 110)* A final phase of the development will include an office complex for Bell Canada (Parkin Partnership, 1982) and, eventually, residential buildings.

The development already covers what were five city blocks. Two former cross-streets have been closed, their original locations marked among four major entrances to the complex at Dundas Street, Trinity Mall, Albert, and Queen streets. Seen from Yonge Street, the entrances help to divide the massive project visually; inside, they widen to facilitate connections between street and underground levels. *(Figures 111, 112)*

Unlike Robson Square, the Eaton Centre's exterior does not create a narrative sequence. Instead of rising from a beginning to a climax with episodes along the way, it is consistently eventful and diversified throughout its considerable length. The two towers are similar in detail, but their slightly offset positions at opposite ends of the Galleria respond to the landmarks and streets that make up their immediate context. Along Yonge Street, the porcelain-enamelled skin of the new Eaton store (E.L. Hankinson with associate architects Parkin Millar & Associates; Bregman & Hamann as consulting architects and structural engineers) folds in and out around its columns, distinguishing it from the grey and white cladding of the rest of the Centre, while emphasizing its similarly massive scale.

The Centre's various entrances and shop-front details, also framed prominently with structural members, impart an image of controlled diversity. Along the western, rear wall of the Eaton Centre, which will eventually be hidden behind the final developments of the master plan, a frankly industrial use of materials reveals a rationally organized megastructure. The individuality of commercial outlets is therefore only perceived along Yonge Street. *(Figure 113)*

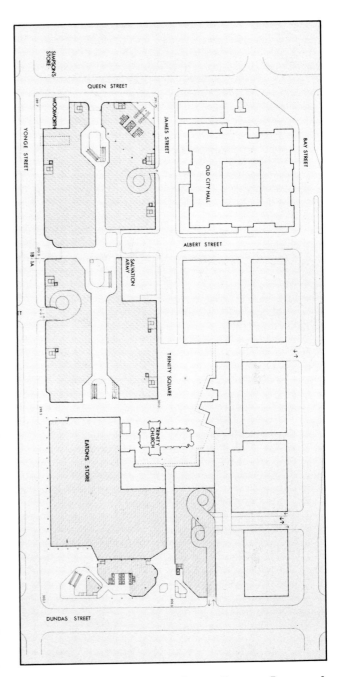

Figure 110. Site Plan of Eaton Centre, Toronto. Bregman & Hamann and the Zeidler Partnership, Architects.

Figure 111. Dundas Street entry to the Eaton Centre, inside the glass entrance canopy, looking up from the first level below grade. Bregman & Hamann and the Zeidler Partnership, Architects.

The historic Trinity Church, formerly set off on a small square, is now largely surrounded by the back of the Eaton store, its parking garage, and the northern half of the Galleria. The Salvation Army Building (John B. Parkin Associates, 1956) to the south on Albert Street, another local landmark, appears similarly absorbed by the development. The treatment of these buildings is indicative of the problems architects encounter introducing a bland suburban building form (a shopping centre) into a highly differentiated urban site. While the historic buildings are regarded as necessary souvenirs of a more individualized era, the application of current formulas for economic efficiency to construction tends to generalize the context in which those souvenirs are now set. *(Figure 114)*

Figure 112. Eaton Centre. Entrance to the Galleria, south of the Eaton's store and on a cross axis with Trinity Square.

Figure 113. View of Eaton Centre from Bay Street, the "back" side, just south of Trinity Church.

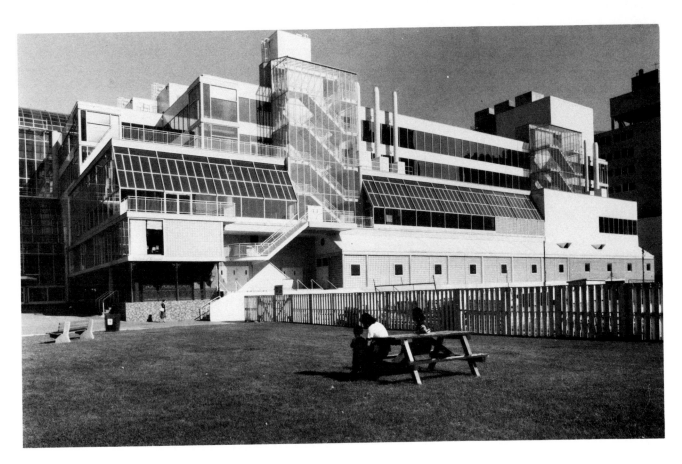

Figure 114. A model of the Eaton Centre complex photo-collaged onto an aerial view of the site, Toronto. Bregman & Hamann and the Zeidler Partnership Architects.

What distinguishes the Eaton Centre from so many other large-scale downtown commercial developments is the linking space of the Galleria mall. Its uppermost level, which contains the most expensive range of stores, has been detailed with awnings and trees planted flush with the floor to resemble a street. As in preservation projects discussed in the previous chapter, the top-lit passage of the Galleria gives new value to mid-block space, and makes it habitable year-round. Within the limits of commercial mega-development, the Eaton Centre Galleria creates a sense of place both on the scale of the individual, with benches and gardening, and on the city scale, with connections to subways, and to a lesser extent, streets. *(Figures 115, 116)*

Figure 115. Eaton Centre. Inside the Galleria, looking south
to the Queen Street entrance.

Figure 116. The Yonge Street facade of the Eaton Centre, showing the use of stair towers, steel structure, balconies, benches and lights to create a scale appropriate to the pedestrian life of Yonge Street. Bregman & Hamann and the Zeidler Partnership, Architects.

By consolidating six hectares (fifteen acres) of downtown land into a single parcel, the Eaton Centre's consortium client (Cadillac Fairview Corporation, the T. Eaton Company Ltd., and the Toronto-Dominion Bank) has indeed gentrified a formerly sleazy strip of Yonge Street. But the design elements that make the Centre a hospitable rather than a hostile presence on Yonge Street were effected partly through the political pressures exerted on the developer by municipal politicians. At their urging and in exchange for permitting street closures, the Centre provides such positive urban design features as shopfronts on Yonge, access at the former street locations, and concealment of the parking garage that fronts onto Yonge Street. The success of the Centre as an urban place bears testimony to the importance of making civic as well as commercial priorities articulate.

Place Desjardins, Montreal

Like the Eaton Centre consortium, the backers of the Complexe Desjardins selected a derelict site in Montreal's downtown core for a development to combine high-rise office space with a variety of commercial facilities.

The developer of Complexe Desjardins is the Desjardins Cooperative Movement, a group of Quebec credit unions *(caisses populaires)* and affiliated trust and insurance companies together with the then-Liberal provincial government. Although the venture was ostensibly independent of party politics, it pointedly symbolized the ascendance of French-Canadian initiative in the Quebec economy. As Claude Ryan pointed out in a 1976 *Le Devoir* editorial, the pressure on the developer to succeed was made greater by the fact that the *caisses populaires'* financial growth was founded on the savings of *"les petits gens."*

The Desjardins group used the prominence of its 3.2 hectare (eight-acre) site to promote the venture. By assembling and rebuilding on all properties from Ste. Catherine south to Dorchester Boulevard and between Jeanne-Mance and Saint-Urbain streets, the developers promised they would create "the concrete symbol of a fierce determination to remodel the city, and thereby, the man on the street."

The replacement of the tightly-packed, low-rise brick buildings with the huge new concrete Complexe was to be the architectural analogue of the transformation of Québecois society by the *Révolution Tranquille.*

The site was aligned, on a north-south axis, with the historic Place d'Armes in Old Montreal, and the Place des Arts complex of theatres (Affleck, Desbarats, Dimakopoulos, Lebensold, Michaud and Sise, 1963), both of which are subway stops. The Complexe Desjardins in fact has access to the Place des Arts station via a tunnel under Ste. Catherine. *(Figures 117, 118)*

The Complexe Desjardins consists of two principal parts. The first is the Complexe, which is made up of four high-rise buildings set on a continuous three-storey podium, or *basilaire*. The podium takes the place of the former low-rise commercial buildings, all traces of which were removed.

Figure 117. Aerial view of Complexe Desjardins, Montreal. La Société la Haye-Ouellet, urban design.

Figure 118. Exterior of Complexe Desjardins, viewed from Place des Arts, Montreal.

The second part is Place Desjardins, a covered, climate-controlled .4 hectare (one acre) area in the centre of the podium. Surrounded by shops, bank branches and restaurants, Place Desjardins is an open space of roughly the same size as Place d'Armes. It is one storey below street level, but is connected by escalators to a street-level Promenade that runs through the middle of the Complexe from north to south. *(Figure 119)*

As an indication of its fierce determination to make Place Desjardins work, the management established an Animation Service to work full-time co-ordinating activities. Groups can schedule displays on such diverse subjects as art, astronomy, or the environment. Tapings for live radio and TV shows are a regular feature. The monthly spectacular, *"Les Vendredis de la pleine lune,"* is one of the Animation Service's most popular activities, featuring live performances by Québecois singers and entertainers. Unlike Eaton Centre, Place Desjardins has Muzak, coloured floodlights, and other accoutrements typical of suburban shopping plazas. It has been defended by local architects and critics as an expression of anti-elitist cultural aspirations. *(Figures 120, 121)*

The Complexe is much harder to like than the Place. Its four pre-cast concrete towers (three for offices, one for the Méridien Hotel) rise out of the podium near, but not at, the four corners of the block. They are not artfully aligned, like Mies van der Rohe's Westmount Square in the heart of Montreal's wealthiest English-speaking residential district, to suggest different sculptured compositions when viewed from afar. Nor are they consolidated into a single, recognizable emblem like I. M. Pei's cruciform Place Ville Marie, several blocks away at the nerve centre of the anglo business district. The Complexe's architects grouped the four towers clockwise in order of height. The shortest, the hotel, is across from the grassy corner of Place des Arts; the tallest two, at thirty-two and forty-one storeys respectively, face the traffic of Dorchester Boulevard. This pinwheel arrangement of the towers reinforces the existing segregation of pedestrian and vehicular traffic: the buildings are lowest across from the park where there are the greatest number of pedestrians, and highest where there are the greatest number of cars, along Dorchester. Visitors must enter the podium to gain access to the offices above but, once inside the Complexe, it is difficult to locate the elevator cores buried within the labyrinth of retail outlets.

Determined to hire French-Canadian architects, planners, and engineers for the development, the Desjardins Movement and its partners, the Société de Développement Immobilier du Québec (SODEVIQ) rejected the widespread practice of the big Canadian banks of importing established American architects to design their corporate headquarters. Because of this practice, few local firms had had experience in planning and designing projects of such complexity and magnitude. Ultimately, the project lacks the single-minded stylishness typical of Canadian bank headquarters.

Complexe Desjardins was master-planned by one urban design firm, La Société La Haye-Ouellet, and designed in segments by a team of local architectural firms. Longpré, Marchand, Goudreau did the podium and the infrastructure for the Complexe; Blouin Blouin joined Gauthier, Guité, Roy to design the three office towers; and Jean Ouellet and Jacques Reeves, of La Haye-Ouellet, designed the Méridien Hotel. Janin Construction supervised the construction, and four consulting firms were involved in the structural and mechanical engineering.

Jacques Reeves, a partner in the architectural firm Ouellet and Reeves, comments that Place Desjardins is one of the few spaces in the project to survive the design/management process in more or less original form. "When you have two architects working on something," he observes, "if one presents the idea of doing something square, the other will obviously want to make it circular, because the pride of the firm is not to be dictated to, but to find a unique solution." Critical of the office towers' design, he was also disappointed by the materials and finishes used for the Place: "The most successful part of the Complexe is the size — not the treatment — of the interior Place. The nicest Complexe Desjardins is the one that's in the drawers."

Figure 119. Complexe Desjardins, Montreal. Escalator down to Place in foreground.

Figure 120. View of temporary photography exhibit in the Place (wood sculpture by the escalator by Pierre Grange, is a permanent installation).
Figure 121. Place Desjardins during Full Moon Friday spectacular.

Many of Montreal's public squares are of humble origin. St. Louis Square, initially a reservoir, was converted to a park in 1880 when houses were built around it. Place Victoria was a hay market, Dominion Square a cemetery, and Viger Square a swamp used as a repository for dust swept from city streets.

Place Desjardins, however, will probably never attain the international landmark status that early promotional brochures promised: "The Complexe Desjardins will be to Montreal what Times Square is to New York, what the Rond-Point of the Champs-Elysées is to Paris, and what the Picadilly Circus is to London." The social goals of the Place, as combined with the commercial goals of the Complexe, have not been smoothed over with elegant or innovative design. The expression of these goals in a characterless architectural form only points to the subordinate role in which Canadian architects have often been placed by corporate, high-rise development.

Commerce Court, Toronto

Commerce Court in Toronto is an example of a recent large development which successfully provides for private and public interests by assigning them distinct architectural forms (I. M. Pei in association with Page and Steele, 1972). Located at the southeast corner of King and Bay streets, at the "MINT corner," Commerce Court is the headquarters for the Canadian Imperial Bank of Commerce. (MINT is the acronym of the four chartered banks — Montreal, Canadian-Imperial, Nova Scotia, Toronto-Dominion — with high-rise head offices quartered there.) The Commerce's L-shaped site extends south from King to Wellington Street and east from Bay to Jordan Street. *(Figures 122, 123)*

When the Bank of Commerce outgrew its headquarters building at the corner of King and Jordan in the 1960's, it chose not to demolish its office tower but to expand by assembling adjacent property. A timely amalgamation with the Imperial Bank, whose head office was a few doors down on King Street, meant that the bank owned two important corner sites in the heart of the financial district. By 1968, all eight unwanted buildings within the L-shaped assembly, including an architecturally-distinguished branch of the Bank of Nova Scotia, were demolished and parts of Jordan and Melinda streets closed.

The decision to keep the Commerce's old office tower (York & Sawyer in association with Darling and Pearson, 1931) proved to be a key move. The finely-detailed limestone tower set the tone and influenced the scale and relationships of the three new buildings that were to be constructed.

The existing tower was set off by the demolition of an adjoining building, and the base of its western side, formerly a brick party wall, was rebuilt to match the original stonework. A new arched window and door were set into the wall, and the new limestone was selected and carved to match the original. *(Figure 124)*

To differentiate the new tower, Commerce Court West, from the earlier stone building, I. M. Pei placed it so that while both have equal frontage on King Street, the new tower is set back to provide pedestrians an unobstructed view of the historical building's reconstructed west wall.

Figure 122. View, from the east, of Toronto's financial district, photographed when Commerce Court West was the tallest building downtown.

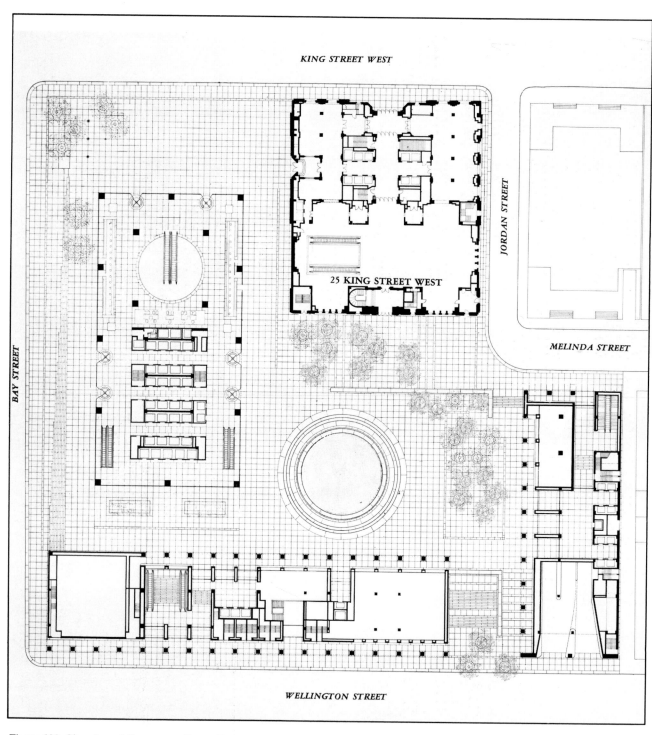

Figure 123. Site plan of Commerce Court, Toronto. All but 25
King Street West by I. M. Pei with Page and Steele, Architects.

This new 57-storey tower, like the older tower, enjoyed the distinction, when it was first built, of being the tallest building in the Commonwealth and boasted the latest in elevator, insulation, heating and life safety systems. Its curtain wall is made of sheets of stainless steel approximately sixteen metres (fifty-two feet) long, 1.2 metres (four feet) high, and three millimetres (an eighth of an inch) thick. They have "the proportions of a strip of paper," explained Oscar Duskes, the bank's project leader. Every effort, from specially devised finishes for the steel to the use of special suction machinery to lift the panels onto the structural frame without scratching them, was taken to ensure that the glass and steel of Commerce Court West would rise in a perfectly smooth sweep, in studied contrast to the masonry details of the 1931 tower adjacent. The new tower's slightly reflective windows also serve to mirror the older tower. *(Figures 125, 126)*

The other two new buildings (Commerce Court South and Commerce Court East) are clad in large limestone panels to match the older building, and kept relatively low (five and fourteen storeys) to conform to adjacent buildings on Wellington and Melinda streets. All the buildings are grouped around the centrepiece of the development, the outdoor court for which the project was named. The central court is rectangular, with passageways to streets at its four corners. Wide, shallow stairs lead up to the court, gently accommodating the slight rise in elevation of the Bay Street edge, and creating a variety of levels within the granite-paved area. Planted with honey locust trees and featuring a vast circular fountain, the Court is a welcome oasis for the buildings' occupants. The daytime population of the complex is 15,000, the equivalent of a small city. Much larger and better-lit than the narrow streets it replaces, yet more defined and sheltered than the open plaza at the neighbouring Toronto-Dominion Centre, the Court provides an urbane and accessible space well-scaled for its seasonally heavy use. *(Figure 127)*

Victor Ross, the Commerce's official historian, observed that: "In the early days the customer sought the bank, and this simplified the problem of providing premises . . . . With the development of the country and of banking came an increase of competition, and the demand that the convenience and comfort of customers should receive fuller consideration." Commerce Court is perhaps the best example among developer-sponsored public spaces of the "fuller consideration" that must be given if architecture is to address the common good.

Technological changes are largely responsible for the subtle but significant changes bank architecture has

Figure 124. Aerial view of Commerce Court, Toronto.

Figure 125. (left) New Tower, Commerce Court West, Toronto. I. M. Pei with Page and Steele, Architects.

Figure 126. (below) Commerce Court. View of the court looking west, showing the fountain and the West and North towers.

Figure 127. (opposite, above) Commerce Court North (formerly called 25 King Street West). Demolition of an adjoining building exposed the brick west wall, viewed here after being clad in stone to match the other exterior walls.

Figure 128. (opposite, below) The Banking Hall in Commerce Court West.

undergone in recent years. The image of vault-like massiveness and security typical of colonnaded stone banks of the nineteenth century has evolved into a sleek, ethereal aesthetic. This is especially true in Commerce Court's new banking hall, where colossal beams and columns appear to be dematerialized by the faintly lustrous finish of their steel surfaces. Uninterrupted glass walls, glass revolving doors, glass-sided escalators, and light-coloured stone seem to attenuate the building's true mass: the base of the new tower makes tangible the bank's wish to appear accessible.

While the banking hall appears light and even informal, the development consolidates three city blocks that previously accommodated half a dozen different buildings and their respective businesses. Where the compact, fortress-like mass of a colonnaded entry used to be considered to convey stability, today extensive frontage on main streets is the means by which the competitive power of the banks is expressed. *(Figure 128)*

North Vancouver Civic Centre

A renewed concern for the meaning of collective life, although increasingly evident in the large-scale projects, is seen in sharpest focus in institutions recently built in smaller communities. North Vancouver's Civic Centre, the Alberta Government Services Centre, Ponoka, and the St. Boniface Cathedral, Winnipeg, all implicitly address the issues of cultural and architectural continuity on a local, recognizable scale. While not subject to the complex factors involved in the larger urban developments, these modest community institutions nevertheless indicate the extent of new, often conflicting pressures shaping the urban environment.

The use of nature as a point of reference for architecture is typical of west coast design. The tradition of making buildings relate to nature stems from the wooden structures of the Coastal Indians' settlements, and has been modified over the years by the contact Vancouver architects have had with the work of architects on the American west coast, notably those of the San Francisco Bay Area.

Founded and developed primarily for privately-owned houses, the nature-based aesthetic of the west coast has been applied to a public building with considerable success in the North Vancouver Civic Centre (Downs/Archambault, 1974). The Civic Centre bears little resemblance to the sensational, well-groomed Robson Square where landscaping has been imposed on an area of intensely-developed downtown land. Civic Centre architect Barry Downs has attempted to bring out the lush, rugged qualities that dominate the North Vancouver landscape.

Off Lonsdale Avenue between 13th and 14th streets, the new Library and City Hall complex is the present-day centre of gravity for public life in the City of North Vancouver. Founded like other parts of British Columbia on the lumber industry, North Vancouver has always been a quiet residential area. Earlier in the century, activity focussed on the waterfront. Ferries linking the town to Granville (now Vancouver's Gastown district) had their terminals at the foot of Lonsdale. Streetcars carried people up the hill to their homes.

As North Vancouver grew, its buildings spread ever farther up the hillside. Apartment towers climbed the steep and heavily-wooded north shore of Burrard Inlet vying for the best views. New highways and bridges rendered the ferry service redundant and people drove to work and to shop in mainland Vancouver rather than trolleying along Lonsdale. The end of ferry service in 1948 marked the end of the harbour as the city centre. *(Figure 129)*

Figure 129. Archival photo, streetcars and ferry docks at the foot of Lonsdale Avenue in North Vancouver.

Figure 130. North Vancouver Civic Centre, looking towards the mall from Lonsdale. Rectangular wooden frames stand along the Lonsdale sidewalk where 14th street has been closed. Downs, Archambault, Architects.

Figure 131. (below) Mall at upper level of North Vancouver Civic Centre, City Hall to the right, Library to the left.

Figure 132. North Vancouver Civic Centre. Pools and fountains in the mall with City Hall in the background.

Figure 133. North Vancouver Civic Centre. Stairs from lower to upper level of mall. Stairs run parallel to the library wall, at right, which fronts on the upper mall.

When his firm was commissioned to design the new Civic Centre, which was to include both City Hall and the main library branch, Barry Downs assessed the area as formerly "one of old, rustic houses, but today most of them are gone, unfortunately. Towers dominate the site and walk-ups are all over the place. We wanted the new buildings to look comfortable on their site, and offer most of their ground to civic park space." Thus the two new concrete-frame buildings, like houses in the area, are clad in wood; they are scaled sympathetically to neighbouring low apartment blocks and offer landscaped terraces for the apartment towers to gaze down upon.

The new civic buildings are connected to the shopping area on Lonsdale by an open-air pedestrian mall made by fencing off the part of 14th Street that runs into Lonsdale. London Plane trees and square timber frames, similar to those used as sunscreens on the Civic Centre buildings, stand along the Lonsdale sidewalk where the street has been closed. *(Figure 130)*

The mall follows the contours of an extended fountain, whose terraced pools become wider and more shallow as they near the Civic Centre buildings, an allusion to the mountain streams that are one of the main geographical features of the area. The walls of the low commercial buildings on either side of the open part of 14th Street provide a shield against the ever-present car traffic, creating an informal backyard atmosphere in keeping with the community's relaxed way of life. *(Figures 131, 132, 133)*

The two civic buildings have been sited so that from the lower residential street they present a continuous jagged profile, seemingly growing out of the surrounding hill. Timber sunscreens cover the south walls of both buildings as well as the north wall of City Hall. The west side of City Hall is concealed from an adjacent walk-up by a tall stand of trees, and a berm, sheltering a quiet outdoor reading patio, hides the south side of the Library. *(Figures 134, 135)*

Figure 134. North Vancouver Civic Centre. View of City Hall (left) and Library (right) from lower level of mall.

Figure 135. North Vancouver Civic Centre. View between library (right) and City Hall (left) looking to the stairs in Figure 133.

Figure 136. North Vancouver Civic Centre. Interior of library.

Figure 137. North Vancouver Civic Centre. Interior of City Hall.

Visual and spatial variety inside the buildings is achieved by the irregular placement of walls, clerestory windows, and ceilings. Gerry Brewer, who was Director of the City's Purchasing and Property Services when the Centre was being designed, explained, "We didn't go in for different levels, from good stuff to junk, because we didn't want people confronted with sudden change as they moved through the building — to feel they'd gotten into the Executive branch because there was a carpet on the floor." *(Figures 136, 137)*

Some twenty years earlier, Ottawa, Hamilton, and Edmonton, to name only a few cities, built city halls featuring pod-like council chambers jutting out from typically modern office buildings set in broad, open plazas. By contrast, North Vancouver's Civic Centre, with its council chamber deep at its centre and its exterior sunscreens, blends so thoroughly into its setting that it is easy to drive by without noticing its presence. Its identity as a civic centre can only be sensed, since it has not been symbolized. *(Figure 138)*

Figure 138. North Vancouver Civic Centre. Interior of Council Chamber in City Hall.

The Alberta Government Services Centre, Ponoka

The Alberta Government Services Centre in Ponoka reflects both the graceful natural forms of the surrounding rural countryside and the grass-roots policy of its Conservative client. The provincial government decided to give the sagging profile of the small town, (population, 5000) and that of its own decentralization policy, a boost by locating several of its facilities there in a new building, with the Alberta Opportunity Company as the primary tenant. The Company was set up to make loans to small businesses that cannot secure loans from conventional sources.

The mandate to design a building that would aggrandize the government's presence in the town was implicit. As Ed Clarke, the managing director of the Alberta Opportunity Company, put it:

> The members of the Cabinet said, in effect, to the Department of Public Works, "We want to make a very strong statement. We want to have a dramatic building in this small community of Ponoka to reemphasize to the people of Alberta our commitment to putting operations of the government in small towns wherever it is feasible." So for that reason Doug Cardinal was called in because his qualifications as a dramatic designer I think are well known.

Undeniably dramatic, the Services Centre designed by architect Douglas J. Cardinal is perhaps best described as a series of events, of restlessly fluid forms defying attempts to locate a visual focus. Walls seem to be pulled out of each other, others seem to be drawn right out of the ground, creating the impression of smaller buildings growing out of the larger one. The building's episodic, de-centralized character draws attention to it as a somewhat alien presence in the life of the town. To one side is a commercial strip replete with a 7-Eleven store; on the other is a street of modest wood-frame houses. Facing the Centre is another street of wooden houses, while behind it, across a lane, is the local lumber yard.

The customary design solution of providing a principal facade, to be regarded from one static, central position, was ruled out from the start. "One facade," says Doug Cardinal, "would [have made the building] look like a train, a three-storey train. By pulling stairwells and forms in and out, when you walk down the sidewalk, you get a series of experiences, rather than just one — blah — government building experience." *(Figures 139, 140)*

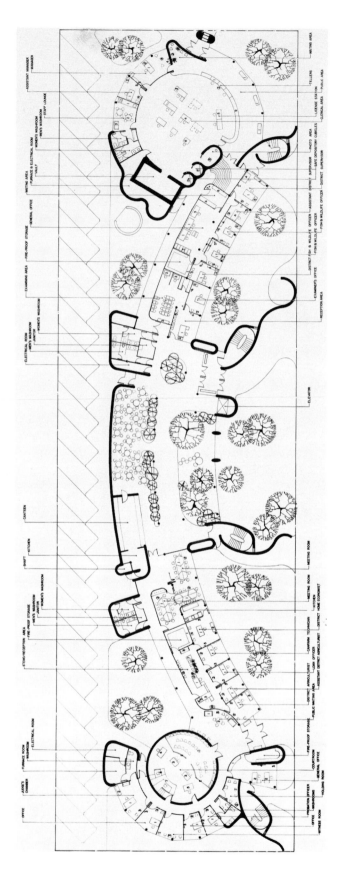

Figure 139. First Floor Plan of Alberta Government Services Centre, Ponoka. Douglas J. Cardinal, architect.

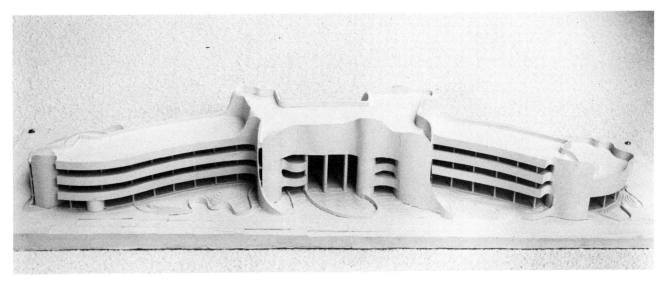

Figure 140. Model of Alberta Government Services Centre, Ponoka.

At either end of the building two cylindrical pavilions curve tantalizingly away from view. Inside, both pavilions are perfectly circular in plan, with ceilings formed like a wheel with spokes radiating out from a hub. The western one is a court room. Here the centre point is the place where the accused and counsel sit. The eastern pavilion, which faces the commercial strip, is a branch of the Alberta government credit union. As in the court room, the visitor's glance is drawn to the centre of the space, but here tellers, not the accused, occupy the central area.

Outside, the cylindrical forms of the pavilions blend into the undulating main body of the building. The back and front form a continuous, over-all facade, inverting the typical function of end pavilions. In Neoclassical institutional buildings, end pavilions tend to draw attention to the monumental aspects of the central hall, while in Cardinal's building, their effect is to deformalize the entire structure. Furthermore, Cardinal's symbolically introverted forms belie the fact that most of the building's interior is devoted to quite ordinary government office space, grouped around a quite ordinary, though curvilinear, central atrium. *(Figures 141, 142)*

Structurally, the curvilinearity of the Alberta Government Services Centre would have been most easily executed in concrete, and it would have been in keeping with local building conventions to have used stucco as a finishing material. But Cardinal sought instead to approximate the limitless subtlety one finds on the Prairies as the sun passes over the narrow range of colours and forms. And so, to make the building's surface more analogous to the natural surroundings, and despite the difficulties it posed for construction, the architect insisted on cladding it in variegated brick, which changes colour with the weather, and throughout the day as the sun strikes it from different angles. Thus it is difficult to attribute a single nature to this building, or to take its measure with a single glance.

Unlike the simply-constructed traditional buildings of the Prairies, such as the grain elevators at the foot of the street Cardinal's building sits on, the Government Services Centre has been achieved with an astonishing array of technological props, from computers to Crazy Glue. Computers facilitated the complex calculations necessitated by the irregular structural forms, and Crazy Glue was applied to keep recalcitrant bricks in place. The result is a structure quite different from vernacular buildings of the Prairies which, like the grain elevators, most often make their presence felt as acts of defiance to the subtly amorphous nature of the landscape. By contrast, Cardinal's unorthodox building looks as though it had been blown and eroded into shape by natural forces. *(Figure 143)*

Figure 141. Exterior of Alberta Government Services Centre, showing steps leading to main entrance of the government offices. Douglas J. Cardinal, architect.

Figure 142. Alberta Government Services Centre, Interior, atrium.

Figure 143. The Alberta Government Services Centre, view of
Ponoka from sidewalk beside the Treasury Branch.

St. Boniface Cathedral, Winnipeg

The evolution of a community's cultural traditions is epitomized by the reconstruction of St. Boniface Cathedral, the fifth cathedral to be built on a magnificent site facing the Red River in Manitoba's main French-speaking settlement. The first cathedral was built of logs in 1819 by Father Provencher, the first Bishop of Western Canada. The second, larger cathedral was destroyed by fire in 1860. The third cathedral was the scene of Louis Riel's funeral in 1885, and was demolished after the fourth and largest cathedral, a Tyndall limestone structure, was completed directly behind it. Riel, who was born in St. Boniface, is buried in the graveyard in front of the fourth cathedral, beside his relatives the Lagimodières, the first white family to settle in Western Canada. Foundation stones from the corners of the third cathedral are still visible amongst the graves. In 1968, workmen repairing the roof of the sixty-year-old building inadvertently started a fire which quickly gutted the body of the basilica, leaving only the outer walls and fragments of the curved wall of the sanctuary. *(Figure 144)*

When, in 1970, the City of St. Boniface was amalgamated with other communities to form a "unicity" government for Winnipeg, many citizens feared that their long-standing control over their French-speaking institutions was in jeopardy. This sudden secular change followed the more gradual ecumenical ones introduced by Pope John XXIII's Second Vatican Council, which

started in the early sixties. These changes involved fundamental transformations of Roman Catholic liturgy that were meant to inspire a direct, fraternal relationship between man and God in the religious service, by de-emphasizing the elaborate intermediary symbols which had evolved over the centuries.

By the time of the 1968 fire, the diocese recognized that the building would have to be altered to accommodate the new, democratized liturgy. Although only the outer walls were left, many people, nevertheless, were tempted to build the cathedral anew. However, by 1970, the cost of an accurate reconstruction proved beyond the reach of the congregation, which was only half as large as the one for which the old cathedral had been built. They chose the firm of Etienne J. Gaboury and Associates to make proposals for a replacement.

While the way in which the cathedral was rebuilt reflected the community's quest to implement the directives of the Second Vatican Council, it also represented a significant change in its architect's approach to the design of religious buildings, and perhaps to architecture generally. Etienne Gaboury, a Franco-Manitoban architect who has designed all types of institutional buildings in St. Boniface, is perhaps best known for his

Figure 144. A view across the Red River to the stone frontispiece of the old St. Boniface Cathedral, St. Boniface, Manitoba.

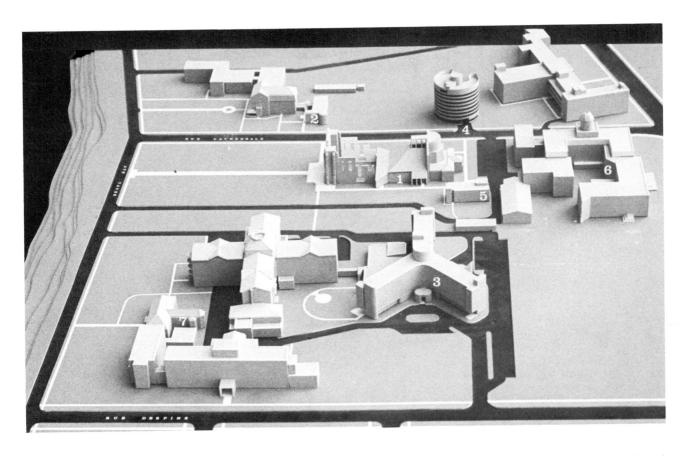

religious buildings such as the Paroisse du Précieux Sang (Precious Blood), which radically altered the way people experienced religious services. The unusual formal organization of his churches — the plan of Precious Blood is spiral — jolted the congregation into direct, often austere, relationship to the religious service.

In the case of the St. Boniface Cathedral, however, the idea of removing the former building's traces so as to build a smaller, modern cathedral would have meant going backwards historically, in that previously, each successive cathedral built on the site had been larger than its predecessor. It was imperative, as far as Etienne Gaboury was concerned, to incorporate fragments of the former building in a contemporary cathedral. *(Figure 145)*

One can still approach the building by entering the white, wrought-iron gate on Taché Avenue, and continuing along the sidewalk that bisects the graveyard. At the end of the sidewalk rises the limestone facade of the old Cathedral. The turrets of its towers were destroyed in the fire, making the highest point the cross at its centre. Below the cross, the circular opening of a former rose window startlingly reveals the sky, and, gradually as one continues along the sidewalk, the vast, rusted steel roof of the new building. *(Figure 146)*

Figure 145. Model of the Diocese of St. Boniface, numbered buildings have been designed or renovated by Etienne Gaboury. No. 1 is the St. Boniface Cathedral.

Figure 146. St. Boniface Cathedral. A frontal view of the old cathedral's face, the roof of the new cathedral seen through the opening of what was once a rose window.

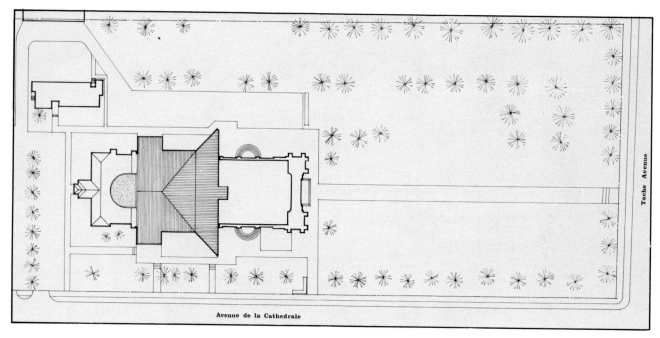

Figure 147. Site plan of the St. Boniface Cathedral reconstruction. Shaded area shows extent of roof of the new cathedral. Etienne Gaboury, Architect.

Figure 148. Main Floor Plan of St. Boniface Cathedral reconstruction.

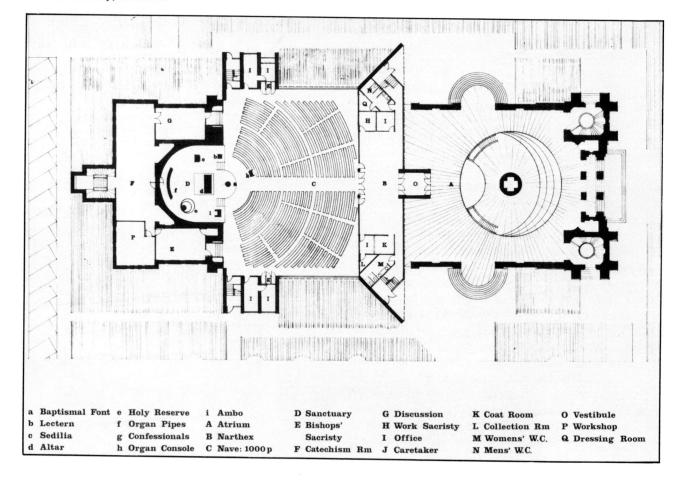

a	Baptismal Font	e	Holy Reserve	i	Ambo	D	Sanctuary	G	Discussion	K	Coat Room	O	Vestibule
b	Lectern	f	Organ Pipes	A	Atrium	E	Bishops'	H	Work Sacristy	L	Collection Rm	P	Workshop
c	Sedilia	g	Confessionals	B	Narthex		Sacristy	I	Office	M	Womens' W.C.	Q	Dressing Room
d	Altar	h	Organ Console	C	Nave: 1000 p	F	Catechism Rm	J	Caretaker	N	Mens' W.C.		

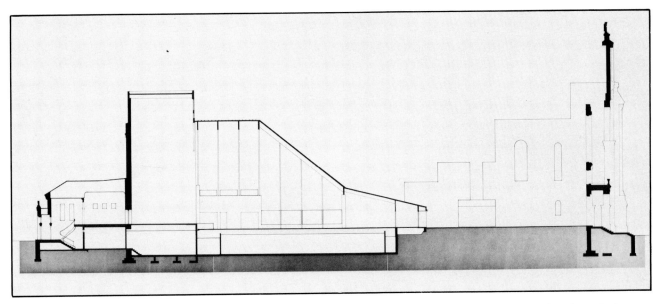

Figure 149. St. Boniface Cathedral. Section through the new building showing its relation to the remains of the old.

The long, narrow dimensions of the former building did not readily lend themselves to a contemporary Roman Catholic church service — ideally, a square or circular space where the congregation gathers in an intimate and uncomplicated relationship to the altar. Taking both the long processional route of the old, and the compact space of the new into consideration, Etienne Gaboury inserted a square contemporary cathedral into the well-preserved sanctuary still standing at the rear of the site. The area between the back of the impressive, now windowless front wall of the old cathedral and the modest low front wall of the new cathedral was retained in its roofless fragmentary state. This outdoor courtyard now functions as a lobby, a sheltered space for the socializing that precedes and concludes religious services. *(Figures 147, 148, 149)*

In this courtyard, the relationship between the old and new cathedrals becomes clear. Where once there were aisles, there now stand six new column-like objects of the same self-rusting steel as the new cathedral's roof. The self-rusting steel, evoking the structure that was destroyed in the fire, symbolizes the common properties of the ruin and the new buildings, as do the large blocks of stone which have been rescued from the old walls and placed randomly, as benches, before the threshold of the new cathedral. These elements help to make the courtyard a place of transition between the former cathedral's ceremonial approach and the more domestic qualities of the new building. *(Figures 150, 151, 152, 153)*

Rather than revolutionizing the progression of spaces inside the new cathedral as he had in previous churches, Gaboury modelled the plan after early Roman basilicas in which the relationship between the nave and the sanctuary at the rear is simple and direct. The new sanctuary, wedged into the remnants of the one left standing after the fire, retains its simple cylindrical form. The square-shaped body of the building accommodates a glassed-in porch-like reception area (the narthex) and the cathedral proper. Gone is the traditional choir loft with its long row of confessional booths underneath. The choir, when it is present, joins the rest of the congregation, sitting in pews at the front. Confessionals are small office-like rooms projecting out from both sides of the body of the cathedral. The apse, where the long axis culminates, has been cleared of the many devotional and immobile objects that typically furnished sanctuaries in nineteenth-century churches. *(Figure 154)*

Neither an exact replica nor a revolutionary statement about the building it replaced, the new St. Boniface Cathedral holds great cultural significance for its community. It is a work of restraint, reflecting the persistence of local traditions while representing current practice in Catholic worship. Like the Alberta Government Services Centre and the North Vancouver Civic Centre, the Cathedral bears witness to the aspirations of the community it serves.

Figure 150. St. Boniface Cathedral. Exterior view of new cathedral and of side entrance to courtyard through ruined wall of the old. Etienne Gaboury, Architect.

Figure 151. St. Boniface Cathedral. View back across courtyard to frontispiece of the old cathedral.

Figure 152. St. Boniface Cathedral. View from ruined stair tower across the courtyard to the new cathedral.

Figure 153. St. Boniface Cathedral. View of courtyard and new cathedral.

Figure 154. Interior of new St. Boniface Cathedral, St. Boniface.

A growing recognition of the value of inner-city sites and existing buildings is in evidence in much of the new construction in Canadian cities. Comparison of these community-scale projects with the same architects' work of the 1960's — aggressively isolated projects like the Simon Fraser campus by Arthur Erickson and Geoffrey Massey, (Burnaby, B.C.), Douglas Cardinal's St. Mary's Church, (Red Deer, Alberta), Eberhard Zeidler's McMaster Health Sciences Centre, (Hamilton, Ontario), Etienne Gaboury's Precious Blood Church, (Winnipeg, Manitoba) — show how profound the re-evaluation of urban design has been.

In buildings and projects of widely differing scales, these architects have abandoned many of the reductive characteristics of the immediate post-War period. In moving away from the earlier goal of producing neutral backgrounds adaptable to every function, architects are making specific accommodations for the shifts in contemporary culture.

V Change and Continuity: Towards a Reconciliation

More and more in recent years, have we seen profound criticism and questioning of the precepts of International Style architecture. While many talented and well-established architects find it convenient to label all alternative approaches "Post-Modernism," and to condemn them as effete and socially irrelevant, the fundamental facts are that the International Style has been damaging to the urban environment and that the public continues to find it, on the whole, unengaging and uninspiring.

Moving beyond the "two-camps" approach of Modernism and Post-Modernism, which remains a superficial explanation of current architectural thought, many architects have attempted to combine the sometimes conflicting aims of the founding ideals of Modern Architecture with the more recent movements towards a socially and environmentally conservative architecture. Architecture, in this case, is intended to be neither strikingly new, nor purely a reflection of that which went before, but to occupy a middle ground between the two.

As part of this trend, a new Canadian architecture is emerging. Its creators draw on the freedom of forms, materials and spaces inherent in the idea of a modern architecture, while also responding to the existing physical and cultural context. Some of the best of these buildings are discussed in this chapter. They bode well for the future: here is an architecture not only optimistic and forward-looking, but also firmly rooted in local and public traditions.

Museum of Anthropology, Vancouver

Not many of Arthur Erickson's buildings are good examples of this recent trend. Canada's best-known architect views much of today's culture as "trash-oriented," and therefore ignores it. As a result, many of his large urban projects, such as Vancouver's Robson Square and Toronto's new Roy Thomson Hall, seem detached from their surroundings. But, where Erickson does value the context, he responds quite differently and carefully to the surrounding environment. A case in point is his design for Vancouver's Museum of Anthropology (Arthur Erickson Architects, 1975).

Perhaps more than anything else, Arthur Erickson is enamoured of the richness and beauty of the British Columbia landscape. His Robson Square suggests a lush, eventful, natural landscape in the middle of downtown Vancouver. Such efforts, however, were unnecessary in the magnificent natural setting acquired for the Museum of Anthropology. Perched on the Point Grey Cliffs of the campus of the University of British Columbia, the rear of the site affords a panorama of Howe Sound below, and the mountains of the North Shore in the distance. *(Figure 155)*

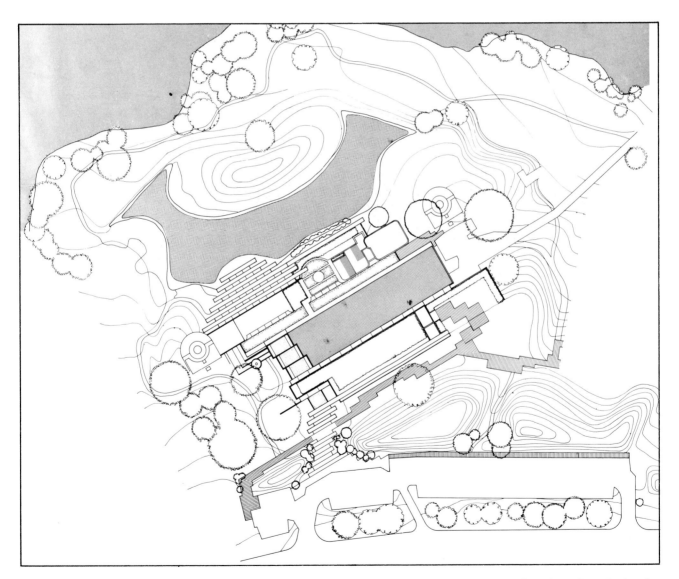

Figure 155. Site Plan, Museum of Anthropology, University of British Columbia, Vancouver. Arthur Erickson, Architect.

From the parking lot, however, the vista is almost completely concealed by a large berm. A chunk of this vast earthwork has been removed to reveal the museum's grand front entrance. Like the berm, which conceals most of the building only to reveal and emphasize its entrance, the museum conceals and then reveals the site as the visitor passes through. *(Figure 156)* "Since the site is sloped," explains Erickson of the way the building structures the visitor's passage through the site, "I felt that the whole movement should be down a long ramp, with more and more revealed, until the whole space burst open with a view of the sea."

From the lobby a carpeted ramp, lined with larger-than-life Northwest Coast Indian wood statues, leads down to the rear of the building. At the bottom, the passageway suddenly opens up into the dramatic, windowed Great Hall, where the museum's extraordinary collection of totem poles stands against a backdrop of forest, water and mountains. *(Figures 157, 158)*

Figures 156, 157. Museum of Anthropology, the grand front entrance (above) and (below) a carpeted ramp which leads down to the rear of the building.

Figure 158. Museum of Anthropology. Interior view of the Great Hall: ". . . down a long ramp . . . until the whole space burst open with a view of the sea." (Erickson).

Figures 159, 160. The major structural theme of the museum recalls the forms of the early Haida houses.

Built to house the University of British Columbia's sizable collection of Northwest Coast Indian art, the Museum of Anthropology reflects in many ways the artifacts it contains. "When I was designing the museum," explains Erickson, "I remembered a photograph of an early Indian village between the edge of the forest and the edge of the sea." Accordingly, Erickson created a path for a river at the rear of the site, and located not only his building but also two of the museum's recreated Haida log houses along it. (The pebbled path has yet to be filled with water because of environmental objections raised by the university.)

Looking back from the rear of the site at the Great Hall and the two Haida houses, the first and most obvious relationship is in the resemblance between the simple and powerful forms of the museum and those of the houses. A closer look at the museum and the culture of the Northwest Coast peoples reveals other, more subtle similiarities. *(Figure 159)*

Beginning at the entrance, the visitor is introduced to the major formal or structural theme of the building. The museum is constructed of a series of frames or

Figure 161. Museum of Anthropology, looking inland at the Great Hall: architecture which structures and heightens the visitors perceptions. Arthur Erickson, Architect.

gates, each unit consisting of a horizontal beam supported by two vertical posts. Although a single gate or frame would have marked the entrance to a typical Northwest Coast Indian log house, in the museum they are used in sets; three, for instance, are used to create the main entrance to the building.

Each of these frames has a carefully-differentiated front face and side profile, a distinction also important to the art of the Northwest Coast Indians, wherein animals are traditionally painted either in full face or side profile according to which view is thought to best portray a creature's most salient characteristics. The face of the shark, for example, is always shown from the front, fully capturing its powerful teeth. The raven, with its pronounced beak, is almost always shown in profile. In the museum, the face of each gate — the plane through which one walks — is represented by a deep beam sitting on two slender piers; the side of the gate reveals the narrow "U"-shaped profile of the beam, resting on two wide piers. Together, these individual gates provide the museum as a whole with a face

and a profile, like a person, or a thunderbird for that matter. *(Figure 160)*

The culmination of the museum in the Great Hall is as grand from the outside as it is from the inside. Looking back at the museum from the rear of the site, the gates or frames have been arranged so that all of them will be visible. Although each gate is distinct, not one of them could be removed without destroying the overall unity of the group. Again, a parallel can be drawn with Northwest Coast Indian art, where the true forms of animals are often distorted to conform to the limits of the picture plane. Totem poles, for example, are built up out of a number of discreet, but interdependent parts. *(Figure 161)*

Few visitors fail to be moved by the museum. On the surface, it is a cool and pristine building in contrast to its lush setting and unusually animate artifacts. Fundamentally, however, the architecture of the museum structures and heightens the visitor's perceptions both of British Columbia's grand landscape and of its Northwest Coast Indian Art.

Pavilion '70, The Laurentians, Quebec

Architecturally ambitious and site sensitive, Pavilion '70 (Righter, Rose and Lankin, 1976-8) is a ski chalet located an hour north of Montreal in Quebec's Laurentian Mountains. Like the Museum of Anthropology, Pavilion '70 has an architectural character appropriate to its function. *(Figure 162)*

Movement through Pavilion '70 is casual and lacks the processional character of a walk through the museum, but there are similarities in the way that the two buildings contract and expand according to external circumstance. The side of Pavilion '70 facing the parking lot is compact and condensed *(Figure 163)*. A central recessed door leads into an unremarkable central hallway lined with metal lockers for skiers. A large stair on the left leads up and out to the main floor of the building. There a central hall gives way to a semicircular, exterior court opening out towards the ski slopes at the rear of the site.

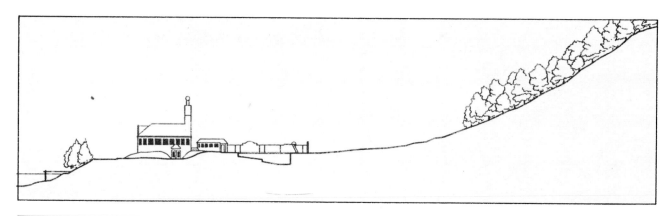

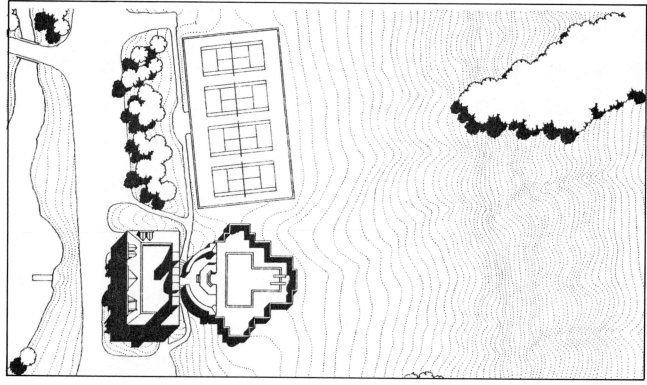

Figure 162. Site Plan and Site Section of Pavilion '70, a ski lodge in the Laurentians an hour north of Montreal. Righter, Rose and Lankin, Architects.

Figure 163. Pavilion '70, elevation facing the parking lot with the ski-hill rising behind.

Figure 164. Pavilion '70, elevation facing the slopes, the symmetry of the facade and the semi-circular court provide an image both grand and inviting. Righter, Rose and Lankin, Architects.

To skiers gliding down towards it, Pavilion '70's symmetrical wood-clad facade presents an image of grandness that belies the actual size of the building. Visual interest is focussed at the centre of the building, on the chalet's formal exterior court and entrance. The semi-circular court serves as a transitional area, a bridge between the scale of the ski-hill and that of the lodge's interior. The curved wood arcade, which defines the court, houses a continuous bench which is warmed by radiant heaters concealed within the uppermost part of the structure. Skiers use these seats at the beginning and end of their day, to put skis on and take them off. Those who prefer not to risk a broken leg or frostbite have a perfect perch from which to watch. A balcony off the second floor bar provides both a canopy and a rather theatrical platform from which to observe the forecourt below and the ski-hills above. *(Figure 164)*

There is something familiar but also exotic about the form of the lodge: it is, at once, a barn, a Quebec manor house and an Italian villa. Wood is the primary structural and cladding material, and it is also used wherever the hand comes into contact with the building, for doorpulls, interior wainscotting, moulding and trim. Pastel colours in recesses throughout the building contrast with the natural wood surfaces of the main walls, imparting an interesting, layered effect to much of the interior. An easy charm pervades the pavilion, and the building is an accommodating and colourful host to the skiers who come from all over the world to use it. *(Figures 165, 166)*

Figure 165, 166. The easy charm of Pavilion '70's interior.

Gaslight Square, Vancouver

In a rural setting, architectural issues are easier to isolate, and architectural ambitions tend to be less compromised than in an urban one. In cities, sites and constraints are tighter, and political influences are more complex. As discussed previously, urban buildings are often designed by committees, and unfortunately often tend to look that way. Urban buildings which conserve and enhance their surroundings, without either disappearing into them or overpowering them, are rare. Four such buildings are discussed below.

As of the mid-60s, the plan for much of Vancouver's waterfront could be summed up by the term Project 200. Conceived as a way of upgrading one of the city's most run-down areas, Project 200 was named for its estimated cost, in 1965, of $200 million. A project of this magnitude was only possible because of Marathon Realty's ability to make available the CPR railyards along Vancouver's waterfront, which it owned, to a development consortium, Project 200 Properties.

Associated with Project 200 was a highway planned to cut through the old waterfront district and adjacent Chinatown. Both the highway and Project 200 provoked considerable protest from citizens' groups. An alternative proposal prepared by the architectural firm of Birmingham and Wood, argued in a detailed and persuasive way for retention and restoration of the historic waterfront district of Gastown. Some new businesses and shops had recently established themselves in the area and some renovation was already underway. With encouragement from city council, the province declared Gastown an historic site, thereby putting an end to the possibility of indiscriminate demolition in the area.

By 1973, Project 200 had been scrapped. But rather than sell its historic block of buildings on Water Street, the consortium chose to hire the firm of Henriquez and Todd to prepare a redevelopment plan for that block alone.

Henriquez and Todd presented a three-stage development plan for the almost 180-metre-long (approximately 600-foot-long) Water Street block. In the first stage, an empty lot in the middle of the block was to become a public square. The new square would be defined by the two existing warehouse buildings flanking the lot, and by a new retail and office building placed between the lot and the street. In the second stage, the block's other buildings were to be restored and new signs and awnings installed. The third phase called for the renovation of upper floor warehouse spaces for use as offices and housing to meet expected demand. *(Figure 167)*

For the public square, the client initially envisioned a ''U''-shaped building, its forecourt opening onto the street in the manner of a typical suburban shopping mall. The architects disagreed, however, insisting that such a solution would destroy the continuity of the existing buildings' facades.

Now determined to do the right thing for the community, Project 200 Properties consented to the Henriquez and Todd design for the square. Rather than the broad opening to the square envisioned by the client, the architect's design called for a carefully defined courtyard entered through a small gap between the facades of the new and old buildings. Completed by 1975, and named Gaslight Square, the three-building complex maintains the continuity of the street's facades, as well as the integrity of the block and area generally.

The street facade of Gaslight Square is dominated by the new building, which is wider and taller than the renovated commercial buildings to either side. Like the existing commercial buildings, the ground floor of the new building features stores with large display windows. Striped canvas awnings shelter the sidewalk in front of the shops. Above the shops is general office space, and a brick facade which features six oriel windows, an unusually-shaped window common to Gastown. *(Figure 168)*

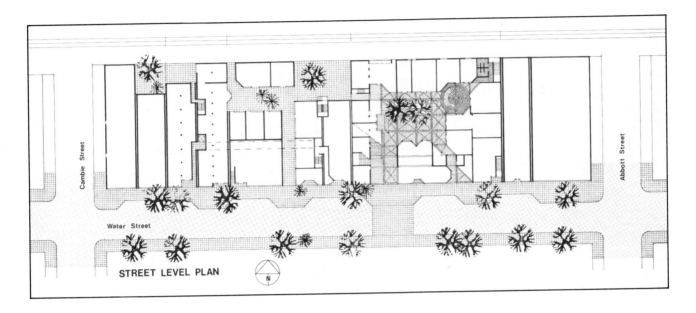

Figures 167, 168. Gaslight Square, Vancouver. (At top) Site plan and (above) Water Street facade. Henriquez and Todd, Architects.

Figure 169. Gaslight Square, the Water Street facade.

Although the materials and forms of the new building are characteristic of the area, the intent of the new, in the words of Henriquez, was to "capture the spirit of what was there without copying it word for word." Thus, some elements have been exaggerated through the manipulation of size and proportion. The "wall-like" quality of the facade has been emphasized by making it wider and flatter than traditional buildings in the area, and through the absence of mouldings and detailed surface decoration. Similarly, the oriel windows are, in relation to the wall, proportionately much bigger than they would be normally. *(Figure 169)*

The square, or courtyard is now sheltered on all four sides: by the new building on the north and south sides, and by the two renovated buildings to the east and west. A walkway encircles the courtyard, gently climbing up and around it, taking the visitor on a gradual spiral tour past the shops inserted into the old structure at the first and second levels. *(Figures 170, 171)*

From its four storey street facade, the new building steps down to two storeys in the courtyard, allowing sun into the square for a longer period of the day. Views of the Burrard Inlet and the North Shore, not possible from Water Street, can be glimpsed from the courtyard's upper walkway. And in contrast to the flat and hard face that the new building presents to the street, the courtyard walls of the complex are veiled and softened by awnings and abundant planting in troughs inserted into the new building's structure. *(Figures 172, 173)*

Figures 170, 171. Gaslight Square, the walkway stepping up and around the courtyard. Henriquez and Todd, Architects.

Figures 172, 173. The courtyard walls of Gaslight Square are veiled by awnings and planting, and enlivened by views of the North Shore. Henriquez and Todd, Architects.

Innis College, Toronto

It was not so much community outrage as a sagging university budget that was responsible for the modesty of the building programme of Innis College in the early 1970s. Established in 1964 as a part of the University of Toronto, Innis College was initially located in a house on Toronto's St. George Street. A few years later, the Toronto firm of Massey Flanders was retained to prepare plans for new facilities on a site along the north side of nearby Sussex Street, between St. George and Huron streets. The Massey Flanders design, approved by the college in 1968, accommodated a projected enrollment of 1500 students, 576 in residence, in a block-long development which featured a ten-storey tower at either end. In proposing to demolish the existing row of Victorian houses along the north side of Sussex Street, and to replace them with a building of a completely different scale, the Massey Flanders scheme resembled the development underway across the street. There, the design for the university's fourteen-storey Robarts Library had required demolition of an entire block. It opened in 1973, and was immediately dubbed "Fort Book" because of its mammoth scale and fortress-like character.

Unlike Robarts Library, the Massey Flanders

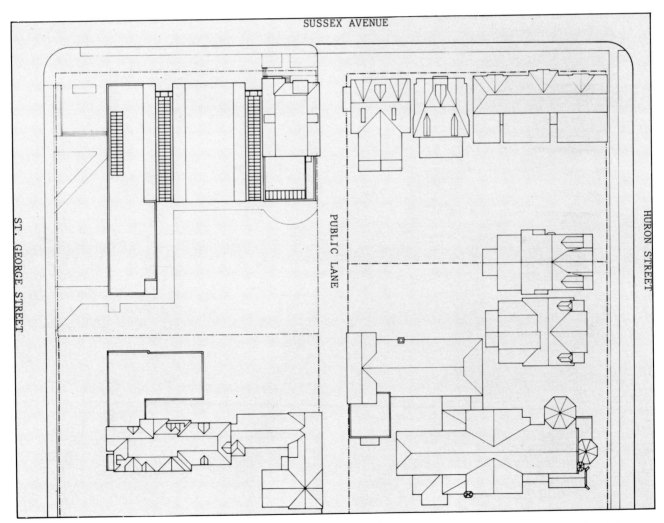

Figure 174. Site Plan, Innis College, the University of Toronto. Diamond and Myers, Architects; Jack Diamond, partner-in-charge.

Figure 175. The Sussex Street facade of Innis College is broken into smaller house-like forms.

scheme fell victim to university cutbacks. In June 1970, John Evans, then the president of the university, advised the college that its new complex could not be built in the "forseeable future." That decision forced a "fundamental rethinking of what the college should be" in the words of Innis College administrator Art Wood, and the college chose to remain small, keeping its projected enrollment to a maximum of 800 students.

Still, Innis required new facilities and a number of architects were interviewed before the Toronto firm of Diamond and Myers was chosen. Chief among the reasons for choosing the firm was its past involvement in community planning and its early advocacy of conservation, re-use and infilling new construction between existing buildings where possible.

In addition, there was the issue of architectural character, the image and atmosphere which would be appropriate for the college. Innis professor Joe Medjuk explains: "One architect, after reading the brief we had prepared, said to us, 'All you people really want is another house,' which was true. We had one old house, and we wanted another but with more stuff in it. As far as this went, Jack [Diamond] knew what we wanted."

As for the site, with a smaller programme and no residential component, less land was required. Both college and architect agreed to preserve the houses still standing on Sussex Street and to design any new structure to blend in with them. "Our first concern," says Joe Medjuk, "was to keep the houses."

Compared to the controversy which attended the opening of Robarts Library across the street, Innis College opened quietly on January 6, 1976. The old houses along the north side of Sussex Street were retained, and one was renovated for use by the college. Attached to this renovated house in an ingenious way is the new part of the college, which extends to the corner of Sussex and St. George streets. From Sussex Street, the complex gives the impression of three "houses," one existing house, and a new building built in two house-like forms. On the larger and busier St. George Street, the image is all new and, in keeping with this street's character, institutional rather than residential. "The first point," explains partner-in-charge Jack Diamond, "was really the restoring of a block, the knitting together of an urban fabric. There were going to be an array of urban elements. [Some never got built.] It wasn't going to be another big building." *(Figures 174, 175)*

Figure 176. Innis College, new building integrated with
renovated Victorian house. Diamond and Myers, Architects;
Jack Diamond, partner-in-charge.

Figure 177. Innis College, glass-roofed walkways join new and old.

The two parts of the new building allude to the Victorian houses next door. They are the same height as the old ones, and, in a rudimentary way, of the same form: brick piers form an arcade reminiscent of the porches next door. Different materials are used on the upper and lower portions of the new building: while the existing house employs brick and shingles, the change on the new building is from brick to clay tile. The simplified roof lines of the new "houses" reflect the steeply pitched gables and intricate dormers of the older houses. By contrast, the shiny, fat aluminum pipes piled deliberately atop the new roof bear little resemblance to

the old brick chimneys next door. *(Figures 176, 177)*

From Sussex Street, the three solid brick buildings are separated by glass-covered walkways which are set back from the brick facades so that they seem, from a cursory glance down the street, not to be there. But the walkways become highly important once one is inside the college. Access to the old house with its classrooms, offices and pub; to the central new building which is called the Town Hall; and to the administrative offices, library, and classrooms, is all via the walkways. People and natural light constantly cross horizontal and vertical paths. *(Figure 178)*

Figure 178. Innis College, access to various parts of the college is through the lively and enjoyable glass-roofed walkways. Diamond and Myers, Architects; Jack Diamond, partner-in-charge.

Figure 179. Innis College, the Town Hall.

Figure 180. Innis College, the library, a quiet, white refuge from the activity of the public walkways. Diamond and Myers, Architects; Jack Diamond, partner-in-charge.

Despite the straightforward organization of the interior, there is a surprising amount of spatial variety, and variety of character within the college. The heart of the college is the Town Hall. In contrast to the carefree skylit walkways that surround it with light and movement, the Town Hall is a brooding, high and dark room. Large white ducts twist under the ceiling, and flare outwards behind the catwalk over a central stage area. Below, the floor's carpeted concentric circles radiate upward from the sunken pool in the centre. "The Town Hall," explains college administrator Art Wood, "was designed to foster oral communication." And it does. "In that room," he continues, pacing back and forth in his small office, "everyone becomes a peripatetic." *(Figure 179)*

The small but airy and open library in the building's "attic" offers a quiet, white refuge from the activity and noise of the public walkways. Here, too, the use of open metal gratings, an architectural theme first introduced in the main stairs, is explored fully and with great beauty. *(Figure 180)*

One of the most popular places in the college, and, in fact, in the university as a whole, is the Innis College Pub. "We asked for a place that could be easily jammed," explains Art Wood, "and that's what we got." Smokey, low and dimly-lit, the new pub incorporates the front room of the renovated house into the college. Lamps, a fireplace and old class pictures lend a comfortably cluttered look to the old room, a dark and mysterious gem which blends in well with the rest of the pub, exemplifying the successful way in which old and new have been combined throughout the College.

Centennial Hall, Winnipeg

Innis College is part of a long tradition of important buildings which have resulted from university commissions. Looking back only so far as the 1960s, Simon Fraser University, Scarborough College, and Massey College each provided initial opportunity and exposure for, respectively, Arthur Erickson, John Andrews and Ron Thom. More recently, the Nova Scotia College of Art and Design has had a large hand in Halifax's waterfront restoration, the University of Toronto has sponsored Innis College, and the newly-formed University of Winnipeg has commissioned the visionary and yet essentially conservative Centennial Hall.

At one time simply a downtown campus of the University of Manitoba, Winnipeg's United College was given a charter of its own in the mid-1960s, and renamed the University of Winnipeg. Expanding enrollment soon necessitated larger facilities, but the newly-chartered institution owned only one block of land in downtown Winnipeg, and that block was already covered, to a large extent, by buildings of various shapes and sizes.

On the south side of the block and facing Portage Avenue, Winnipeg's main boulevard, stands Wesley Hall, a great sandstone monument. Completed in 1896, the Hall was historically identified as *the* college, and later as *the* university. Alongside and behind it are a number of two, three, and four storey buildings of various styles built between 1957 and 1964. Together Wesley Hall and the smaller buildings formed a highly-valued courtyard at the center of the block.

There was one empty plot of land on the block's north end, and that was quickly used for the university's first new building, Lockhart Hall, completed in 1969 by the Winnipeg firm of Moody Moore Duncan Rattray Peters Searle Christie (MMDRPSC). This new brick building, with its picturesque towers, anchored the nor-

Figure 181. Aerial view of University of Winnipeg campus in the late 60's, the sandstone and turreted Wesley Hall facing Portage Avenue at the southern end of the site.

thern end of the campus, complimenting the Neo-romanesque style of Wesley Hall to the south.

The university still lacked adequate classroom space, a proper library, and room to house student services. In total, it required an additional 28,000 square metres (approximately 300,000 square feet). Not only had the last remaining lot been utilized, but 28,000 metres was roughly equivalent to a building three times the size of Lockhart Hall. "Groundspace," recalls Dr. J. G. Pincock, Assistant to the President of the University, "was totally inadequate to erect anything remotely resembling that amount of square footage."

The university's choices were limited. One option was to purchase new land outside of its original block. Although there was an already-assembled, suitably large

site available across the street, its owner wanted double what the university could afford to pay. Another possibility was the selective demolition of some of the lower, newer buildings on the block. But then alternative facilities would have been required while the new ones were going up. With a projected point-of-conception-to-point-of-completion time of two to two-and-a-half years, this option, too, was ruled out. Seven architecture firms were invited by the university to present solutions to this difficult problem. Moody Moore Duncan Rattray Peters Searle Christie (MMDRPSC) was chosen, because it seemed to take the "most imaginative approach."

MMDRPSC proposed a low rise "groundscraper," a "blending" structure that would improve connections between various parts of the campus. As to the location of the groundscraper, "the concept evolved," in the words of James Christie, partner-in-charge, "as an informal system going up, over and around the existing buildings, utilizing the spaces between and above . . . ." *(Figures 181, 182)*

Figure 182. Aerial view of the University of Winnipeg campus with the steel frame of Centennial Hall under construction; the completed brick Lockhart Hall (1969) is at the extreme north of the block. Moody Moore Duncan Rattray Peters Searle Christie, Architects.

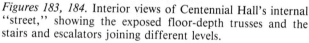

Figures 183, 184. Interior views of Centennial Hall's internal "street," showing the exposed floor-depth trusses and the stairs and escalators joining different levels.

How and where to support the new building? "We had two choices," says MMDRPSC partner Mike Rattray, "either punch down through the existing buildings, or go down over them onto the sidewalk." To disrupt the university schedule as little as possible, the firm opted for the latter, the concept of supporting the building on columns placed on the sidewalk, in front of the existing buildings.

Leaving aside the question of whether the sidewalks *could* be used in this way (they were eventually), the next problem was one of spans between possible supports, spans which ran to thirty-six metres (120 feet) in length. Because engineers recommended two-metre (six-and-one-half-foot) deep trusses, too deep to place in a dropped ceiling without wasting a great deal of space, it was eventually decided to use full-storey trusses. This meant that one floor could be rested on the top chord of the truss, and another hung from the bottom chord, necessitating trusses only every other floor. Thus, two basic engineering concepts, the "stilt concept" and the "full storey truss concept," underlay the complex and radical-looking building which MMDRPSC proposed

for this "little university on this little piece of ground."

Officially opened in September 1972, Centennial Hall, as the new structure has been named, has vastly improved connections between various parts of the campus. Based on an analogy to automobile circulation, where roads vary according to the flow and speed of traffic, a spacious interior pedestrian "street" was created on a north-south axis running through the heart of the new structure and, consequently, the campus as well. In addition to its horizontal function, this "street" has a vertical component: a set of escalators connecting the four floors of the new building in an uninterrupted straight line. Large courtyards are cut out of the building along this spine of escalators, and generous windows allow views out and light in. A trip through this "street" at the heart of the building, which provides access to the rest of the university, reveals overhead a collage of ducts, pipes, exposed three-metre-deep (ten-foot) trusses, interior and exterior spaces, and a series of department store-like exhibits of light, colour and form. *(Figures 183, 184)*

Figures 185, 186. University of Winnipeg, Centennial Hall, the western edge of the site. Moody Moore et al., Architects.

From the outside, futuristic notions of urban design seem to have been combined with the most matter-of-fact and traditional concepts of buildings on streets, sidewalks and courtyards. Clad in dark bronze-finished steel panels, the new building juts out over the sidewalk, beginning at the third storey on one side, and the fourth storey on the other. The walls of Centennial Hall are simply perpendicular to the street, continuing the lines established by the older buildings. Equally important, the new building carefully reinforces the central courtyard. *(Figures 185, 186, 187, 188, 189)*

The Portage Avenue facade of the University of Winnipeg, *the* image of the university to the rest of the city, is considerably strengthened by the addition of Centennial Hall. The grey slate roof of Wesley Hall is pointed up by the dark colour of the new metal building. The symmetrical facade of Wesley Hall, with its twin towers and sloping roof in between, is echoed in the more modern but similarly-formed front of Centennial Hall. Bryce Hall, a small, previously insignificant limestone building, now stands out against a dark metal background. Now more than ever before, the University of Winnipeg presents a handsome, balanced composition of new and old to the rest of the city.

Figure 187. View of Centennial Hall, framed by Wesley and Bryce Halls.

Figure 188. The new building reinforces the existing courtyard.

Figure 189. University of Winnipeg, the Portage Avenue facade — a balance between new and old. Moody Moore et al., Architects.

Citadel Theatre, Edmonton

The site proposed for the Citadel Theatre in downtown Edmonton was in some ways no less difficult than that proposed for Centennial Hall. Not only was the Edmonton site small, but there was an existing garage on its western edge. To complicate matters further, Edmonton's City Planners had proposed a street-level nine-metre-wide (thirty-foot) public walkway to cut through the centre of the site and, eventually, through the theatre itself.

Of five architecture firms invited to submit proposals for the site, the Toronto firm of Diamond and Myers, in association with the Edmonton architect R. L. Wilkin, was chosen for the job. Rather than finding the dimensions and conditions of the site restrictive or daunting, architect Barton Myers saw them as "challenging." "Constraints," he explains, "often become the generators of ideas."

One of the more difficult aspects of theatre design is the strict segregation required between the public "front of house" functions, and the private, production-related functions of the "back of house." Responding not only to this particular characteristic of theatres, but also to the specific nature of the Citadel site in Edmonton, Myers and his associates utilized the proposed walkway as a natural dividing line through the theatre, locating "front of house" functions on one side of it, and "back of house" functions on the other. *(Figures 190, 191)*

Figure 190. Citadel Theatre, Edmonton, the "transparent" west face, corresponding to the "front of house" functions. Diamond and Myers, in association with R.L. Wilkin, Architects; Barton Myers, partner-in-charge.

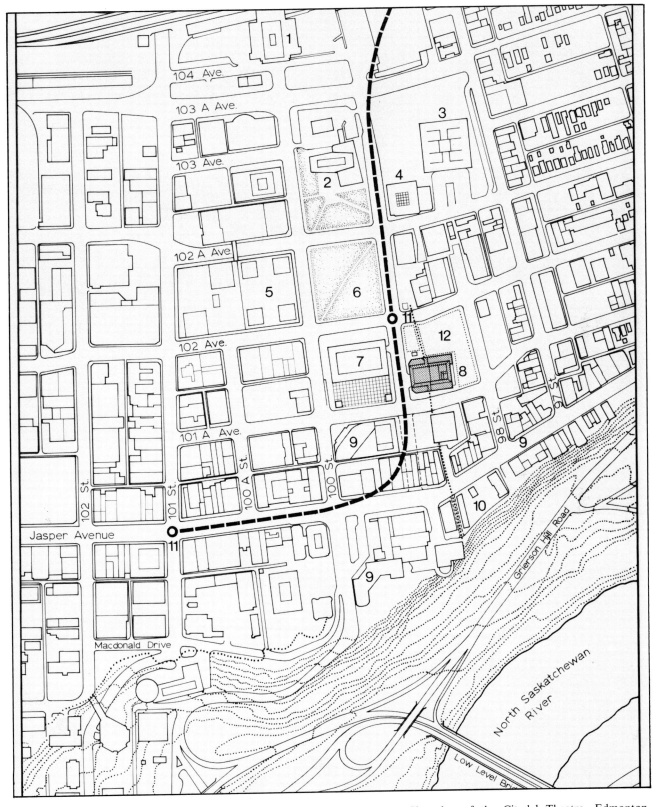

Figure 191. Site plan of the Citadel Theatre, Edmonton.

Figure 192. The walkway, inside the Citadel Theatre complex, from which all three of the complex's theatres are reached.

Figure 193. The comparatively "opaque" east face of the Citadel Theatre, the "back of house." Barton Myers, partner-in-charge.

Opening in 1976, the concept underlying the building's design was that, proceeding along the street-level walkway, one would be able to get a sense of the overall feeling of the theatre, and the location of its constituent parts. Thus, all three of the building's theatres, the Shoctor Theatre, which is the largest, and the Rice and Zeidler theatres, are entered directly from the walkway: the lobby of the Rice Theatre is down a few steps; the Zeidler Theatre is on the same level as the walkway; and the Shoctor Theatre can be reached via a wide, elegant stairway which begins at the walkway. The impact of the Shoctor Theatre on the walkway is especially strong: the stepped underside of that theatre's floor forms the gently terraced ceiling of the walkway itself. *(Figure 192)*

Other openings in the walls of the walkway reveal the Citadel's various public facilities, including its bar, restaurant, box offices and a rather emphatically-lit coat check. The materials of the space are hard and tough: brick walls, tile floor, and concrete ceiling. Appropriately, the walkway seems more an extension of the outside sidewalk than a separate, isolated place.

From the outside, the distinction between "front of house" and "back of house," becomes more evident through the thoughtful and consistent handling of materials. The public "front of house" functions on one side of the walkway are expressed in terms of *transparency*: the front of the building is essentially all glass, a curtain wall. By contrast, those of the private "back of house" are expressed in terms of *opacity*: the back of the theatre is mostly solid brick, its openings punched out only where necessary. *(Figure 193)*

Figure 194. Interior of a rehearsal hall, Citadel Theatre.

Myers' predisposition towards juxtaposing "opposites," whether "metaphysical," in his words, "or purely design devices," is evidenced not only by the transparent/opaque dichotomy of the exterior, but also by equally clear oppositions between front and back created throughout the interior of the building. Towards this end, details and finishes are chosen with extreme care and skill.

With its grey-carpeted floors, and concrete block walls outlined by a poured concrete frame, the "back of house" ranges in feeling from a neutral tone for the office and administrative areas, to the straightforward industrial character of the workshops and rehearsal halls. *(Figure 194)*

Front of house functions, epitomized by the glass-wrapped Shoctor Lobby at the front of the building, are much more plush, colourful and generally more "decorated." The red colour of the Medicine Hat brick, used on the exterior and interior, is echoed in the front of house choice of rust-red carpet and red clay tile floors, burgundy-coloured fabric on the theatre seats, and redwood walls in the Shoctor and Zeidler theatres. While metal window-wall frames have also been enamelled a similar rust-red, other metal fittings, such as stair railings, are brass, creating thin lines and small spots of flash and brilliance within the multi-level, free-flowing space of the central Shoctor Lobby. *(Figures 195, 196, 197)*

Figures 195, 196. Citadel Theatre complex, the lobby and the interior of the Schocter Theatre — "front of house" is plush, colourful and more decorated. Barton Myers, partner-in-charge.

Figure 197. The lobby at night.

Figure 198. Citadel Theatre. Glass arcade on 101A Avenue, one of three arcaded sides of the building.

Viewed from nearby Sir Winston Churchill Square, the squat, red brick theatre with its glass front stands out amidst a surrounding environment of recent, precast concrete buildings which are generally the same on all four sides. The fact that the building does not blend in with its recent neighbors, however, is here a good thing. The front/back dichotomy which accounts for the internal order of the Citadel, also makes sense when one looks at the theatre within a larger urban context. The glass-wrapped front of the building faces onto 99th Street, one of Edmonton's major streets, upon which sits not only the nearby Winston Churchill Square, but also the city's main post office, police headquarters, and the Edmonton Art Gallery. The service-oriented, predominantly-opaque back of the building faces onto the decidedly less important 98th Street.

In deference to surrounding streets, and in hope of re-establishing the traditional, pre-eminent image of streets as volumes — enclosed and defined by the parallel walls of buildings on both sides — the bulk of the Citadel is pushed right up to the sidewalk on all four sides. A glass arcade extends protectively over the sidewalk on three sides of the building. This arcade system, explains Barton Myers, "could easily be incorporated in(to) our cities to make the sidewalk experience less gruesome during inclement weather." *(Figure 198)*

As in Winnipeg's Centennial Hall, an endorsement of traditional and matter-of-fact patterns of urban design has not prevented the designer from tapping the exciting and liberating realm of forms, materials and spaces that remain a positive legacy of the birth of the modern movement. In order to explain the building, Myers refers to his original mandate, that of creating a "warm and theatrical place." Through the juxtaposition of old and new, traditional and modern, a spirit of warmth and theatre pervades not only the Citadel's interior, but also is conveyed through the building's glass face out onto a section of one of Edmonton's most important streets. Of future buildings, in cities across the country, Canadians should demand no less. *(Figure 199)*

Figure 199. The Citadel Theatre at night, a "warm and theatrical place." Diamond and Myers, in association with R.L. Wilkin, Architects; Barton Myers, partner-in-charge.

BIBLIOGRAPHY

Books: —

Acland, James, et. al. *Exploring Toronto.* Toronto: Toronto Chapter of Architects in affiliation with Architecture Canada, 1972.

Affleck, Ray, et. al. *Exploring Montreal: Its People, Buildings and Places.* Toronto: Montreal Society of Architecture in affiliation with Greey de Pencier Publishers, 1974.

Auf Der Maur, Nick. *The Billion Dollar Game: Jean Drapeau and the 1976 Olympics.* Toronto: James Lorimer, 1976.

Baird, George. *Built Form Analysis.* Toronto: City of Toronto Planning Board, 1975.

____. et. al. *On Building Downtown: Design Guidelines for the Core Area.* A Report to the City of Toronto Planning Board. 2nd. ed. Toronto, 1974.

Bernstein, William, and Ruth Cawker. *Building With Words: Canadian Architects on Architecture.* Toronto: Coach House Press, 1981.

Boggs, Jean Sutherland. *National Gallery of Canada, Ottawa, Fifth Annual Review 1972-1973.* Ottawa: The National Gallery of Canada for the Corporation of the National Museums of Canada, 1973.

Butler, Rick, and Jean-Guy Carrier, eds. The Trudeau Decade. Toronto: Garden City; Doubleday, 1979.

Campbell, W., Christian C. Campbell. *Political Parties and Ideologies in Canada.* Toronto: McGraw-Hill Ryerson, 1974.

Chang, Ching-Yu, ed. *Process: Architecture. A Perspective of Modern Canadian Architecture.* With essays by Anthony Jackson, Melvin Charney and A.J. Diamond. Tokyo: Process Architecture Publishing, 1978.

Charney, Melvin. *Oeuvres 1970-1979.* Montreal: Musée d'art contemporain, 1979.

Collier, Robert. *Contemporary Cathedrals.* Montreal: Harvest House, 1975.

Davis, Charles H. *The Vancouver Book.* Vancouver: J. J. Douglas, 1976.

Dendy, William. *Lost Toronto.* Toronto: Oxford University Press, 1978.

Downs, Barry. *Sacred Places: Early Religious Architecture in British Columbia.* Vancouver: Douglas and McIntyre, 1980.

Ede, Carol Moore. *Canadian Architecture 1960-70.* Toronto: Burns and MacEachern, 1971.

Emery, Mark. *Roger Taillibert Architecte-Architect.* Montreal: Editions Hurtibise, HMH, 1976.

Erickson, Arthur. *The Architecture of Arthur Erickson.* Montreal: Tundra Books, 1975.

Fenton, Terry, and Karen Wilkin. *Modern Painting in Canada: Major Movements in Twentieth Century Canadian Art.* Edmonton: Hurtig Publishers in cooperation with The Edmonton Art Gallery, 1978.

Fulford, Robert. *This Was Expo.* Toronto: McLelland & Stewart, 1968.

Gabeline, Donna, Dane Laken and Gordon Pape. *Montreal at the Crossroads.* Montreal: Harvest House, 1975.

Heritage Trust of Nova Scotia. *A Sense of Place: Granville Street, Halifax, Nova Scotia.* Halifax: 1970.

Holm, Bill. *Northwest Coast Indian Art: An Analysis of Form.* 1965. Vancouver: J. J. Douglas, 1978.

Jackson, Anthony. *The Democratization of Canadian Architecture.* Library of Canadian Architecture. Halifax: Tech-Press, 1978.

____. *The Future of Canadian Architecture.* Library of Canadian Architecture. Halifax: Tech-Press, 1979.

Kalman, Harold, and John Roaf. *Exploring Vancouver 2.* Ten Tours of the City and its Buildings. 1974. Rev. enl. ed. Vancouver: University of British Columbia Press, 1978.

Kalman, Harold. *Railway Hotels and the Development of the Château Style in Canada.* Victoria: University of Victoria, Maltwood Museum, 1968.

Lorimer, James, and Evelyn Ross. *The City Book.* With the editors of City Magazine. Toronto: James Lorimer & Company, 1976.

____. *The Second City Book.* Toronto: James Lorimer & Company, 1977.

Morrow, Joyce. *Calgary, Many Years Hence.* Calgary: University of Calgary, 1979.

Nobbs, Percy. *Architecture in Canada.* London: The Royal Institute of British Architects, 1924.

Nova Scotia. Association of Architects. *Exploring Halifax and the South Shore of Nova Scotia.* Toronto: Greey de Pencier Publications, 1976.

Porter, Anna, and Marjorie Harris. *Farewell to the 70's: A Canadian Salute to a Confusing Decade.* Don Mills, Thomas Nelson & Sons, 1979.

Reid, Dennis. *A Concise History of Canadian Painting.* Toronto: Oxford University Press, 1973.

Lehrman, Jonas. "Downtown Winnipeg: A Need for New Goals." *The Canadian Architect,* June. 1975.

____. "Museum of Anthropology: An Appraisal." *The Canadian Architect*, May. 1977.

____. "Vancouver: A Review of Some of the More Controversial Projects." *The Canadian Architect.* Mar. 1972.

Lehto, James, et. al. "Competitions." (Issue on the National Gallery Competition.) *Review of Architecture/Landscape Architecture.* Toronto: University of Toronto School of Architecture. Spring. 1978.

London, Mark. "Montreal's Architecture." *Montreal Star.* 29 Jan. 1977 - 12 Mar. 1977.

Lyle, J.M. "Canadian Architecture." *R.A.I.C. Journal,* Feb. 1927.

MacKenzie, James. "How the 20-Year Political Nightmare of the Spadina Expressway Happened." *The Globe and Mail,* 27 Jan. 1970.

Malcolm, Andrew H. "Montreal Mausoleum: Top Companies Shift Offices to Toronto." *The New York Times,* 2 Sept. 1979.

Marsan, Jean-Claude. "The Van Horne House: Planned Destruction." *Vie des Arts,* Automne 1974.

McConathy, Dale. "Corridart: Instant Archaeology in Montreal." *artscanada,* July/Aug. 1976.

McMordie, Michael. "The Citadel Theatre." *The Canadian*

Forum, Oct./Nov. 1978.

Myers, Barton. "Weighting the Elements." *The Canadian Architect*, Nov. 1977.

Nobbs, Percy E. "Present Tendencies Affecting Architecture in Canada." *R.A.I.C. Journal,* July. 1930.

Parkin, John C. "Architects, Artists and Engineers: Can They Work Together For Space-Age Cities?" *Canadian Art*, Mar. 1965.

____. "Canadian Architecture Since 1945." *R.A.I.C. Journal,* Jan. 1962.

____. "Château and Substance: Towards a Canadian Environment." Address to the Faculty of Environmental Studies, University of Calgary, 28 Oct. 1976.

____. "Relationships: Art in Architecture." Address. July. 1961.

____. "Walter Gropius and Harvard in 1946." Address to the Society of Architectural Historians. Boston, Mass. 27 Jan. 1962.

Rogatnick, Abraham. "Gastown." *The Canadian Architect,* July. 1973.

Sewell, John. "Toronto's Tall and Perfect Mayor Has Something to Say." *Heritage Canada*, Feb. 1979. (Reprinted from *Toronto Life*, Nov. 1978.)

Shadbolt, Douglas. "Postwar Architecture in Canada." *The Canadian Forum,* Apr. 1978.

Smith, C. Ray. "Barton Myers." *Urban Design,* Summer. 1977.

____. "Monochromatic Contextualism." *Progressive Architecture*, July. 1977.

Vastokas, Joan M. "Architecture as Cultural Expression: Arthur Erickson and the New Museum of Anthropology, U.B.C." *artscanada*, Oct./Nov. 1976.

____. "The Montreal Museum of Fine Arts and the Issue of Democratization: Building Versus Collection." *artscanada*, July/Aug. 1976.

Wermenlinger, Daniel, et. al. "Complexe Desjardins." *L'Ingenieur*, Janvier/Février. 1975.

Footnotes

Chapter I

p. 13 "The entire development . . .": as quoted by Robert Fulford in *This Was Expo* (McLelland and Stewart, 1968).

p. 13 "an age of . . ."; ". . . a framework of . . .": Jerry Miller, "Expo 67: A Search for Order," *Canadian Architect,* May, 1967.

pp. 14-15 ". . . choice of . . ."; ". . . free the individual . . .": ibid.

p. 15 ". . . asked to explore . . .": as quoted in "Expo 67: An Experiment in the Development of Urban Space," *Architectural Record,* October, 1966.

p. 18 "At Expo . . .": Robert Fulford, *This was Expo.*

p. 18 "Besides no-space spaces . . .": Jan Rowan, *Progressive Architecture,* June, 1967.

p. 18 "If Canada had . . .": Peter Collins, "Expo — and After," *The Canadian Architect,* October, 1966.

p. 18 "The cannonade of . . .": Peter Newman, *Toronto Star,* April 28, 1967.

Chapter II

p. 21 Despite vigorous protest . . .: The editors of *The Canadian Architect* submitted to a protest letter, signed by 800 architects from across Canada, criticizing the competition procedure to Prime Minister Pierre Trudeau; the Leader of the Opposition; Charles Drury, Minister, Department of Public Works; and Guy Desbarats, Assistant Deputy Minister, Design and Construction. The bulk of *The Canadian Architect's* November, 1976 issue was devoted to the organized protest. See also James Purdie, "Young Architects Out in the Cold Over Plans for New Art Gallery," *The Globe and Mail,* January 24, 1976.

p. 21 . . . eight of the second stage . . .: disclosed during the authors' interview with Guy Desbarats, August, 1979.

p. 21 . . . the kind of cost overruns . . .: In the authors' interview with Guy Desbarats, he explained, "No government can face the loss of control as Australia did in the Sydney Opera House."

p. 23 John Parkin's contact with well-known Modernists: In a letter to Reginald Isaacs, April 8, 1964, John Parkin wrote, "I consider Gropius' example and advocacy the principal influence on my own practice. On my return to Canada, 1947 . . . we consciously set about organizing a firm which would be based upon the team principle involving experts from many interrelated fields." (Letter courtesy of John C. Parkin.) In his address to the Society of Architectural Historians (Boston, Mass., January 27, 1962), "Walter Gropius and Harvard in 1946," John Parkin describes his contacts with well-known Modernists. Of Gropius, Parkin claimed that, "Through Gropius, past Behrens one could reach the very roots of the Modern Movement. For many of us . . . there was a kind of missionary zeal and faith in the new architecture — a faith, I might add, that stood quite inviolate for some, at least until the mid-Fifties. We went to receive a kind of dogma, and to our surprise we found none — only a kind of liberal unitarianism."

p. 23 The Canadian mainstream as pioneers of the post-war period . . .: See Douglas Shadbolt, "Postwar Architecture in Canada," *The Canadian Forum,* April, 1978.

p. 23 . . . second generation of American Modern architects:

See Robert A. M. Stern, *New Directions in American Architecture.* Rev. ed. (New York: George Braziller, 1977.)

p. 23 "Philip said in 1960 . . .": John Parkin, from an interview, with the authors, September, 1979.

p. 24 "This century has overrated . . .": Guy Desbarats, from an interview with the authors, August, 1979.

p. 24 "Architects should be . . .": John Parkin, from an interview with the authors, September, 1979.

p. 24 "Competitions add cost . . .": Guy Desbarats, from an interview with the authors, August, 1979.

p. 24 Jean Sutherland Boggs, the Gallery's Director . . .: Upon Jean Boggs' appointment as Director in 1966, Judy La Marsh, then Secretary of State, announced in the House of Commons, "She is the first woman to head an agency with the status of Deputy Minister." Jean Boggs authored a history of the Gallery in 1971, *The National Gallery of Canada.*

p. 24 Jean Boggs campaigned . . .: See the *Ottawa Citizen,* May 2, 1972.

p. 24 . . . the taint of a political gesture . . .: In late 1974, Secretary of State Hugh Faulkner announced that the National Gallery and the Museum of Man would move to Hull, as cultural parallels to the new government office buildings.

p. 24 . . . the Museums Corporation . . .: The National Gallery was grouped with the National Museum of Natural Science, the National Museum of Man, and the National Museum of Science and Technology.

p. 25 . . . Jean Boggs left Ottawa . . .: See Adele Freedman, "The Mess at the National Gallery," *The Globe and Mail,* June 7, 1979; Letters to the Editor, "National Gallery no 'mess,' doing its best," *The Globe and Mail,* June 16, 1979.

p. 25 ". . . an illustrated book . . .": Prof. G. S. Vickers, from an interview with the authors, September, 1979.

p. 25 ". . . doing the adjacencies . . .": Fred Rounthwaite, from an interview with the authors, September, 1979.

pp.. 25-27 "I didn't even recognize . . .": C. Blakeway Millar, from an interview with the authors, September, 1979.

p. 27 . . . most ambitious . . . objective of the programme: This important objective was Item 4C - 2 - 02.11.9 of the Project Programme.

p. 27 "The building had almost . . .," "Taking cognizance of . . .": Boris Zerafa, from an interview with the authors, September, 1979.

p. 27 "Architecture is not an opening night . . .": John Parkin, from an interview with the authors, September, 1979.

p. 30 By his own account . . .: from the authors' interview of Boris Zerafa, September, 1979.

p. 30 "We certainly felt . . .": ibid.

p. 30 ". . . its major virtue . . .": The jury's final report, from which this and subsequent quotes have been taken, is reproduced in the appendix in its totality, as required by the Department of Public Works.

p. 32 "Then, finally, there was . . .": John Parkin, from an interview with the authors, September, 1979.

p. 32 ". . . leisurely ability to go . . .": ibid.

p. 34 . . . jury's point of view: See the interview with I. M. Pei in *American Architecture Now.* Ed., Barbaralee Diamonstein. (New York: Rizzoli, 1980.) ". . . this museum [the East Wing of the National Gallery] should not really be a large museum but should be broken down into a series of small museums . . ."

p. 34 "There was a very clear . . .": Prof. G. S. Vickers, from an interview with the authors, September, 1979. See also Mary McAlpine, "A New Home for the Nation's Art," *The Vancouver Sun,* April 6, 1977.

p. 36 "When you place a heap . . .": Raymond Moriyama, from an interview with the authors, September, 1979.

p. 38 "I. M. Pei is a purist . . .": Victor Prus, from an interview with the authors, August, 1979.

p. 38 "It's very difficult to relate . . .": I. M. Pei as quoted by Barbaralee Diamonstein in "I. M. Pei: 'The Modern Movement is now wide Open,'" *ART News,* Summer, 1978.

p. 40 Wellington Street was viewed . . .: See *Review of Architecture/Landscape Architecture,* University of Toronto, Spring, 1978.

p. 42 . . . the architects of Centre Pompidou . . .: See Suzanne Stephens, "Future Past," *Progressive Architecture,* May, 1977.

p. 43 "In terms of contemporary . . .": C. Blakeway Millar, from an interview with the authors, September, 1979.

p. 43 For a discussion of the trend away from the monumentality characterized by Pei's museums, see Paul Goldberger, "What Should a Museum Building Be?" *ART News,* October, 1975.

p. 43 "I'm a medievalist . . .": Prof. G.S. Vickers, from an interview with the authors, September, 1979.

p. 44 "You might see a Picasso . . .": Paul Cravit, from an interview with the authors, September, 1979.

p. 47 "The architects on the jury . . .": Prof. G. S. Vickers, from an interview with the authors, September, 1979.

p. 47 "Any strong architectural . . .": Gustavo da Roza, from an interview with the authors, September, 1979.

p. 49 "At last the director . . .": T. Morris Longstreth, "Early Hardships of Canada's Great Art Collection," February 25, 1933. This clipping was found by the authors, marked "no source," in the Metropolitan Toronto Library's Fine Arts Vertical File — Ottawa. National Gallery of Canada.

p. 49 In 1954, the first competition . . .: See "Plan Competition to Pick National Gallery Architect," *Ottawa Evening Journal,* May 5, 1952; "List Archives With Best Plans for Art Gallery," *The Globe and Mail,* October 22, 1952; "Winnipeg Architects Win National Gallery Design," *Ottawa Citizen,* March 2, 1954.

p. 49 . . . the gallery's staff and collections moved . . .: For details of the move, see "National Art Gallery Closing Till January," *The Globe and Mail,* July 4, 1959; "Gallery Open Unofficially — For Rats," *Toronto Star,* December 11, 1959; "National Art Gallery Battles Rats," *Toronto Star,* December 14, 1959.

p. 49 . . . a temporary haven . . .: See "National Gallery on Elgin Street," *Ottawa Journal,* February 15, 1955; "An Art Gallery on Elgin Street," *The Ottawa Citizen,* February 16, 1955.

p. 44 The public has grown increasingly . . .: An excellent account of the Gallery's decline can be found in Geoffrey Stevens' series of articles in his *Globe and Mail* column, "A National Disgrace," January 13, 1981; "A Gallery in Retreat," January 14, 1981; "A Depressing Saga," January 15, 1981.

p. 49 . . . Public works has quietly pursued . . .: Gyde Shepherd, from an interview with the authors, February, 1981.

p. 49 Director H'sio Yen-Shih resigned: See Adele Freedman, "The Mess at the National Art Gallery," *The Globe and Mail,* June 7, 1979; Adele Freedman, "100th Birthday Celebrated in Fine Style," *The Globe and Mail,* March 8, 1980; John Gray, "Head of National Gallery Resigns Over Budget," *The Globe and Mail,* November 12, 1980; Adele Freedman, "The National Gallery Flounders in Red Tape," *The Globe and Mail,* November 22, 1980.

p. 49 ". . . lack of good faith . . .": Ronald Dick, from an interview with the authors, September, 1979. See also Kay Kritzwiser, "Architects Assemble their Plans for New National Gallery," *The Globe and Mail,* April 25, 1977.

p. 50 "Most of the entries . . .": Guy Desbarats, from an interview with the authors, August, 1979.

p. 50 "The competition process seems . . .": Gyde Shepherd, from an interview with the authors, August, 1979.

p. 50 "Artists have special visions . . .": Dr. H'sio Yen-Shih, quoted by Sandra Peredo, "Art and Taxes," source unknown.

p. 50 When Parliament received a request . . . to spend $885,000 . . .: Robert Duffy, "PM's Phrase About Paintings Has a Contemptuous Ring," *The Globe and Mail,* December 20, 1958. Of interest in this issue is the story of Joseph Hirshhorn's art collection. See Sol Littman, "Oh, the art they've lost for us!" *The Toronto Star,* January 7, 1979.

p. 50 "Historically, the last century . . .": John C. Parkin, "Relationships: Art in Architecture," a speech delivered in July, 1961.

p. 50 ". . . the days are gone . . .": I. M. Pei, as quoted by Barbaralee Diamonstein in *American Architecture Now.* (New York: Rizzoli, 1980.)

p. 50 ". . . new social . . .": John C. Parkin, "Relationships: Art in Architecture," a speech delivered in July, 1961.

p. 50 "The legal responsibility . . .": John Parkin, from an interview with the authors, September, 1979.

p. 51 "If we have no great . . .": John C. Parkin, "Château and Substance: Towards a Canadian Environment," a speech delivered to the Faculty of Environmental Studies at the University of Calgary, October 28, 1976.

p. 51 ". . . a great architect, artistic . . .": from an interview with the authors, September, 1979.

p. 51 ". . . concrete symbols of pride . . .": Guy Desbarats, from an interview with the authors, August, 1979.

Chapter III

p. 57 "Imaginatively restored . . .": submission from The Committee of Concern and the Heritage Trust of Nova Scotia, to the mayor and city council, 1968 (courtesy Allan Duffus).

p. 57 "These buildings are . . .": from an advertisement placed in *The Halifax/Herald Mail Star,* June, 1969.

p. 57 "The response was . . .": Allan Duffus, from a letter to the authors, June, 1978.

p. 60 "Houses and stores . . .": as quoted in *A Sense of Place: Granville Street* (The Heritage Trust of Nova Scotia, 1970), p. 6.

p. 70 "People don't appreciate . . .": John Clarry, as quoted in "Harbourfront: $200 Million Gamble," *The Toronto Star*, June 14, 1980.

p. 71 ". . . an idea . . . that the 91 acres . . .": in *Planning Principles* (Harbourfront Corporation, October, 1980.)

p. 72 ". . . un-project-like . . ."; ". . . the virtual stuff . . .": Michael Kirkland, from an interview with the authors, January, 1981.

p. 74 "We wanted to . . .": Norman Hotson, as quoted by Adele Freedman in "Former Swamp Now Painted and Peopled," *The Globe and Mail*, December 6, 1980.

p. 75 ". . . randomness, curiosity . . .": as quoted by Michael and Julie Seelig, in "Granville Island," *Architectural Record*, September, 1980.

p. 77 ". . . a red carpet . . .": *Montreal, Olympic City* (COJO, 1976). p. 91.

p. 77 "I noticed that . . .": Jean Drapeau, as quoted by Nick Auf der Maur in *The Billion Dollar Gamble: Jean Drapeau and the 1976 Olympics* (Toronto: Lorimer, 1976).

p. 79 ". . . some giant Paleozoic . . .": John Hix, "The Velodrome," *The Canadian Architect*, September, 1976.

p. 79 ". . . often the case . . .": Paul Sandori, "Olympic Complex: Structural Development," *The Canadian Architect,* September, 1976.

p. 80 "We were beginning . . .": Melvin Charney, from an interview with the authors, August, 1979.

p. 80 "Money is all . . .": Roger Taillibert, as quoted by Nick Auf der Maur in *The Billion Dollar Gamble.*

p. 80 "The design is . . .": Jean Drapeau, ibid.

p. 80 "The story . . ."; "The budget . . .": Melvin Charney, from an interview with the authors, August, 1979.

p. 81 "The mindless strip . . ."; ". . . the original sense . . ."; ". . . with a history . . .": Melvin Charney, "Corridart on Sherbrooke Street" (COJO, 1976).

p. 82 ". . . regrettable failure . . .": Jean Drapeau, as quoted in "What Happened when the Mayor Took a Drive Down Sherbrooke St.," *The Gazette*, October 6, 1979.

p. 82 "Tomorrow's architecture . . .": *Roger Taillibert Architecte — Architect*, Roger Taillibert with Marc Emery, (Hurtibise, HMH, 1976).

p. 82 ". . . necessity of architecture . . .": Melvin Charney, from *Vanguard*, March 1977.

p. 83 ". . . the public content . . .": Melvin Charney, from an interview with the authors, August 1979.

Chapter IV

p. 87 The post-war policies of the Central Mortgage and Housing Corporation: See James Lorimer, *The Developers.* (Toronto: Lorimer, 1979).

p. 91 "Plus 15 has had . . .": Harold Hanen, from an interview with the authors, July, 1979.

p. 95 Town planner Thomas Mawson . . .: See Joyce E. Morrow, *Calgary Many Years Hence.* (Calgary: University of Calgary, 1979.)

p. 96 Toronto, too, had planned . . .: For a detailed account, see K. Greenberg, "Toronto: The Unknown Grand Tradition," *Trace*, vol. 1, no. 2, 1981.

p. 100 "I got the T.T.C. and Yorkdale . . .": Hans Blumenfeld, from an interview with the authors, September, 1978.

p. 106 "Justice must not . . .": Arthur Erickson, quoted in "Vancouver's Dazzling Centre: Arthur Erickson Designs an Airy, Elegant Masterpiece," *TIME*, October 1, 1979.

p. 108 "Our surroundings, most . . .": Arthur Erickson, from an interview with the authors, July, 1979.

p. 112 What distinguishes the Eaton Centre: See Peter Collymore, "New Atria of Canada," *The Architectural Review*, vol. 167, no. 999 (May, 1980).

p. 115 As Claude Ryan . . .: See Ryan's editorial, "Le complexe Desjardins, et après," *Le Devoir*, 5 avril 1976.

p. 115 By assembling and rebuilding . . .: See Mark London, "Lessons to Learn in Giant Complexe," *The Montreal Star,* March 12, 1977.

p. 115 ". . . the concrete symbol . . .": Quoted from "Le Complexe Desjardins — Un bref historique," translation by the authors. (Brochure courtesy of the Service d'Animation, Place Desjardins.) See also Wendie Kerr, "Return to Former Status Sought for Montreal," *The Globe and Mail*, June 2, 1979.

p. 116 Place Desjardins been defended . . .: See Jean-Claude Marsan, "For a Cultural Architecture in Quebec," *Building With Words.* Eds. William Bernstein and Ruth Cawker. (Toronto: Coach House Press, 1981). See also Melvin Charney, "The Montrealness of Montreal," *The Architectural Review*, vol. 167, no. 999 (May, 1980).

p. 116 Complexe Desjardins was master-planned . . .: For details of the planning process, see: Daniel Wermenlinger, et al., "Complexe Desjardins: Planification et Réalisation," *L'Ingénieur*, Janvier/Février, 1975; Jean-Claude La Haye, "La Place Desjardins Sans Complexe," *Le Devoir*, April, 1976; Marc Lessard, "Un complexe comme nous autres," *La Presse*, 7 avril 1976.

p. 116 "When you have two architects . . .": Jacques Reeves, from an interview with the authors, August, 1979.

p. 118 . . . Montreal's public squares . . .: See Melvin Charney, "Understanding Montreal," in *Exploring Montreal.* (Toronto: Montreal Society of Architecture in affiliation with Greey de Pencier Publications, 1974).

p. 118 The social goals of the Place . . .: See Francine Dansereau, "Two solitudes," *City Magazine*, March/April, 1976.

p. 119 By 1968, all . . . were demolished . . .: For an authoritative account of buildings demolished to make way for new bank headquarters, see William Dendy, *Lost Toronto.* (Toronto: Oxford University Press, 1978).

p. 119 . . . 25 King Street West (the 1931 tower) . . .: For contemporary impressions of the tower at King Street West, see: "Details of the New Head Office Building," *Caduceus* (Courtesy of the Canadian Imperial Bank of Commerce Archives); Lt.-Col. Duncan Donald, "The Why and Wherefore of the New H.O. Building," *The Caduceus*; For details of the Commerce Court tower, see *Canadian Building*, August, 1972.

p. 121 ". . . the proportions of a strip of paper . . .": Oscar Duskes, from an interview with the authors, September, 1978.

p. 121 "In the early days . . .": Victor Ross, *A History of the Canadian Bank of Commerce.* Toronto, 1922.

p. 123 The image of vault-like . . .: William Dendy, "Temples of Commerce: From the First Canadian Bank to the Second World War." (Courtesy of William Dendy). See also A. Bruce Etherington, "Bank Design: A Progress Report," *The Canadian Architect*, March, 1964.

p. 124 Founded and developed . . .: See Rev. Wm. Scott, "The Early Story of North Vancouver," Museum & Art Notes, Second Series, The Art, Historical and Scientific

Association of Vancouver, B.C., March, 1950.

p. 126 ". . . one of old, rustic houses . . .": Barry Downs, from an interview with the authors, July, 1979.

p. 128 "We didn't go in for . . .": Gerry Brewer, from an interview with the authors, July, 1979.

p. 130 "The members of Cabinet . . .": Ed Clarke, from an interview with the authors, June, 1979.

p. 130 "One facade," says . . .: Doug Cardinal, from an interview with the authors, June, 1979.

p. 134 . . . a "unicity" government . . .: See Cecil Rosner, "Unicity Idea a mistake, planner says," *Winnipeg Free Press*, February 19, 1977.

p. 134 . . . fundamental transformations of Roman Catholic liturgy . . .: From an interview with Dr. Badertscher, Professor of Theology, Winnipeg . See Etienne J. Gaboury, "Design for Worship," *The Canadian Architect*, March, 1968.

p. 135 Precious Blood Church: See Jonas Lehrman, "Precious Blood Church," *The Canadian Architect*, October, 1969.

Chapter V

p. 145 ". . . trash-oriented . . .": Arthur Erickson, from an interview with the authors, July, 1979.

p. 146 "Since the site . . .": Arthur Erickson, as quoted by Edith Iglauer in "Seven Stones," *The New Yorker,* June 4, 1979.

p. 148 "When I was designing . . .": ibid.

p. 148 Northwest coast Indian art . . .: see *Primitive Art*, Franz Boas (Dover, 1955).

p. 160 ". . . forseeable future . . ."; "fundamental rethinking . . .": Art Wood, from an interview with the authors, February, 1981.

p. 160 Credits for Innis College are: Diamond and Myers, Jack Diamond, partner-in-charge.

p. 160 "One architect . . .": Joe Medjuk, from an interview with the authors, September, 1978.

p. 160 "Our first concern": ibid.

p. 160 "The first point . . .": Jack Diamond, from an interview with the authors, August, 1978.

p. 165 "The town hall . . .": Art Wood, from an interview with the authors, September, 1978.

p. 165 "We asked for . . .": ibid.

p. 167 "Groundspace was . . .": Dr. Pincock, from an interview with the authors, May, 1979.

p. 167 "most imaginative approach": ibid.

p. 167 ". . . blending" structure . . .": ibid.

p. 167 "The concept evolved . . .": James H. Christie, "University of Winnipeg," *Western Construction and Industry,* August/September, 1972.

p. 168 "We had two choices . . .": Mike Rattray, from an interview with the authors, May, 1979.

p. 168 ". . . stilt concept . . ."; ". . . full-storey truss concept . . .": Dr. Pincock, from an interview with the authors, May, 1979.

p. 168 ". . . little university . . .": Mike Rattray, from an interview with the authors, May, 1979.

p. 172 Credits for the Citadel Theatre are: Architects: Diamond Myers and Wilkin. Design: Barton Myers and R. L. Wilkin. Implementation: Barton Myers Associates and R. L. Wilkin Architects.

p. 172 ". . . challenging . . ."; "Constraints often . . .": Barton Myers, from a letter to the authors, September 1978.

p. 176 " . . . opposites," whether "metaphysical, . . .": Barton Myers, "Weighting the Elements," *The Canadian Architect,* November 1977.

p. 178 ". . . could easily be . . .": ibid.

p. 178 ". . . warm and theatrical place . . .": Barton Myers, from a letter to the authors, September, 1978.

Index

APPENDIX

BOARD OF ASSESSORS' REPORT

NEW NATIONAL GALLERY OF CANADA LIMITED ARCHITECTURAL COMPETITION

MARCH 11, 1977

The Board of Assessors wishes to express its awareness of the honour and responsibility inherent in its appointment to assess the submissions presented by ten teams of competitors for the Limited Architectural Competition for the new National Gallery of Canada. We express our thanks to Public Works Canada, and especially to Mr. Guy Desbarats its Assistant Deputy Minister, as well as to the staff of the National Gallery of Canada, for the facilities and help with which they have eased our task.

All submissions presented to our review preserved the condition of anonymity, being identified only by a letter and number designation. The programme for the competition, as prepared by Philip Bobrow and Associates Ltd. for Public Works Canada as documentation for the competitors, had been available to members of the Board of Assessors for several months before its meeting. Public Works Canada had assessed the submissions on purely objective points, with several technical committees for such criteria as fulfillment of mandatory requirements; for the handicapped, users' and functional needs, performance and specifications. Reports of these committees were, however, not considered by the Board of Assessors until the last phase of its deliberations. We are grateful to members of the National Capital Commission and staff of the National Gallery of Canada who have contributed to the technical committees.

Preamble

The mandate entrusted to the Board of Assessors is to select an architect for the National Gallery of Canada (letter from Guy Desbarats, 14 October 1976, to the competitors) by assessing the competitive designs on a conceptual basis (programme, p. 23, 2J-1.04a).

In exercising its mandate the Board of Assessors followed certain general criteria that it considers fundamental to the project.

1. The National Gallery of Canada serves as the repository and custodian of those manifestations of man's creativity that form the nation's cultural heritage and demonstrate Canada's place in the history of civilisation. As such its physical container must express a presence that honours and dignifies its functions.

2. The National Gallery of Canada will be sited in the heart of the National Capital, extending the link between legislative, judicial and cultural functions of government as expressed physically in Parliament Hill, the Supreme Court complex and itself. It must respect the urban complex developing on Wellington Street West, as well as the typical Canadian landscape of the Ottawa River and its stony escarpments.

3. The National Gallery of Canada is a meeting-place for people and art. This can be achieved only in an environment which will meet a certain number of requirements. The working functions of the institutions are specified in the programme. In addition, its architectural design must welcome the visitor with a clear demonstration of accessibility and comprehensibility. Its form, structure and relationship of parts must help the visitor to become receptive of and familiar with art.

4. The National Gallery of Canada will be constructed with public funds, its costs must, therefore, be controllable and efficiently deployed.

Assessment

The Board of Assessors has decided that submission 4567890123 (hereinafter referred to as "H") is the best conceptual design among the ten competitors.

After review of all ten submissions the Board of Assessors determined that only one of two possible routes of judgment was possible. Selection of the design with the least number of faults could not lead to an acceptable design. On the other hand, selection of the one with a major virtue presents a potential for a distinguished effective and sound structure.

"H" distinguishes itself from the other competitors by its sense of order. Three components play an important role in its effect — measured proportions, structural clarity, and its diagonal location on the site. The structure's symbolic value is identifiable. At the same time its relationship of external form with internal space could be exciting. Its sense of order is an interesting beginning to an integrated solution, and should allow the flexibility required to create both "universal space" or spanfree expanses for areas of public congregation and/or special exhibitions, as well as the controlled or disciplined spaces required for activities and permanent collections.

"H" suggests a classic solution to architectural "delight" — subtle, unassertive and rational.

Critique

Urban Design Factor — based on two elements; the axial links between the National Gallery of Canada and the MacKenzie Tower, and the Ottawa business core and beyond the urban surround.

"H" conceives of these links as forming a polarity between their termini. Its diagonal placement should suffice to create a focal interest to those approaching on either axis. The glass screen is unnecessary and distracting. It should be discarded, and the facade restudied with consideration for the interpenetration of spaces. The main entrance should also be reconsidered as to its angular juxtaposition on the axis.

"H" does not attempt to harmonize with other structures adjacent to it. Still, its proposed surface cladding of limestone accords well with the National Archives' granite cladding. In the formal sense "H" is not a good neighbour. However, the Board of Assessors has given serious thought as to whether the immediate urban environment merits an attempt to adjust to it in design, e.g. with the National Archives. Its judgment that the new National Gallery of Canada could create a new standard of architectural design for the area implies that future development of the Wellington Street West locale should be re-energized. Nevertheless, thought should be given to opening views from the National Archives.

The Board of Assessors strongly recommends that, until such time as the Federal Court building is constructed, its site be suitably landscaped. This may be considered an interim solution to correct what might otherwise be seen as an urban wasteland for an indeterminate period of time.

Site Development — based on the following elements; a. natural terrain, b. the river frontage, and c. access and circulation.

a. "H" presents possibilities for the stepping down of its modules or system units to the river; analogy to an Italian hill village presents itself to the art historical imagination. At the same time, the building could include open and closed spaces with different elevations, offering three-dimensional variety when seen from above or below.

b. "H" is not satisfactory in its treatment of the river frontage, but is not incorrectible in this aspect. Thought should be given to the transition between the architectural structure and the river promenade. However, "H" has diagonal views outward, up and down the river, which are potentially the best offered. In addition, its facade seen from the river would offer a dynamic extension of the rugged escarpment forming the base of the Supreme Court.

c. "H" has not solved the circulation patterns on the site; i.e. entrance for tour groups including bus-staging area, servicing of the Cliff Street Plant and the gallery itself, and access to the river promenade.

The Board of Assessors recommends that careful attention be paid to landscaping in terms of natural configurations, as well as selection of plantings.

Design — based on the interior as the ordering system would be reflected on the exterior.

"H" lends itself to a flexible ordering of structure, space and light. At the moment its reception areas are inadequate in space and, therefore, do not suggest the open-mindedness together with indirect signals for orientation that are required for the gallery's presentation to the public. Moreover, its present design does not go beyond a "measure-system." The designer should use its means to create a dialogue between measurements, supports, circulation routes, roof constructions and contrasting spaces. While the ordering system of

"H" could lead to understandable and comfortable spaces, as well as exciting ones, its present rigidity is disturbing to the Board of Assessors. The wells between modules serving only for "circulation bridges" are unnecessary for gallery lighting purposes and useless for activity.

Integrated Systems — based on programme requirements.

"H" generally presents the best thought-out systems among the ten submissions. A number of technical problems remain to be solved — fire-control including exits from stairways, circulation including elevators for visitors, freight (most importantly, works of art) and staff, control of natural light including solar orientation, snow accumulation (most especially on the skylighted roofs), and snow removal in other areas.

The Board of Assessors desires to emphasize that a final design will emerge only in succeeding phases of this project. The essential catalyst for a successful development of the design lies in the future relationship between the architectural team and the gallery's users.

Respectfully submitted to the Professional Advisor, Gordon R. Arnott.

F. T. HOLLINGSWORTH   C.H. OBERLANDER

I. M. PEI   G. S. VICKERS

W. G. QUIST   H. Y. SHIH

Achevé d'imprimer
en septembre mil neuf cent quatre-vingt-deux
sur les presses de l'Imprimerie Gagné Ltée
Louiseville - Montréal.
Imprimé au Canada